"Finding Out For Oneself Is Better Than Being Told"

A Modern East Anglian Man: 1940 to 2000

Mick Wilson

Published by New Generation Publishing in 2021

Copyright © Mick Wilson 2021

First Edition

The author asserts the moral right under the Copyright, Designs and Patents Act 1988 to be identified as the author of this work.

All Rights reserved. No part of this publication may be reproduced, stored in a retrieval system or transmitted, in any form or by any means without the prior consent of the author, nor be otherwise circulated in any form of binding or cover other than that which it is published and without a similar condition being imposed on the subsequent purchaser.

ISBN
    Paperback   978-1-80369-021-6
    Hardback   978-1-80369-022-3

www.newgeneration-publishing.com

Acknowledgements

On a few occasions in the text reference is made to material from the diaries of Mick and Barbara Wilson which have been published previously. I would like to thank John Wiley & Sons Ltd. for permission to site from Wilson B.A. and Wilson M.J. "First Year, Worst Year: coping with the unexpected death of our grown-up daughter" (2004); and to Routledge, Taylor & Francis Group for permission to site from Wilson B.A. "The Story of a Clinical Neuropsychologist: the personal adventures and professional life of a Modern Woman" (2020); and Wilson B.A. "Reaching for Fulfilment for a Woman in Science: further stories of a Clinical Neuropsychologist (2021).

I would also like to thank David Higham Associates for permission to quote the poem St. Thomas Water, Collected Poems (1951) by Charles Causley (MacMillan).

I have quoted a small passage from Trevor Nunn's introduction to Peter Hewett's autobiographical work, "Owlesbury Bottom (The Sumach Press, 1991). I was an adviser to Peter Hewett at the time and am mentioned for my contribution in that book, which is now out of print.

I would also like to commend Bernard Watson, who sadly died many years ago, for his superb family portraits that are included in this book. As you will learn, Bernard was an important member of our jazz band and a well loved art teacher in Ipswich during the nineteen fifties.

This book would not have been written without the advice and support of my wife Barbara; and I'd also like to thank our son Matthew for his assistance in preparing the photographs. I was also encouraged by Tory Dockerill who supported my efforts.

Finally, I'd like to thank the pupils whose written work was originally completed in my classes at Monkwick County Secondary School and published in the school magazines dated 1967 and '68.

List of Figures

Front Cover: Mick Wilson, aged two and eighty-six years

Wilson family in the forties 35

Cross country runners 45

Venice rehearsing 62

CND March 70

Mick playing jazz 72

Drawing of Mick by Bernard Watson 72

Barbara 82

Barbara and the children 104

Barbara 109

Sarah 118

Crossing a bridge 119

Mick after dipping into the river 121

Mick in the canyon 122

Where the raft went in 123

Last picture of Sarah 124

Our ceremony for Sarah 132

Pepé and Barbara in a mild tributary 133

Foreword

I suppose like most authors I have chosen a title for this book after having written the text. This might be the wrong way of doing it? For one reason, choosing the title has made me think again about what I have written and whether I can justify the inclusion of the word 'modern'? I think calling myself 'East Anglian' is justifiable on the grounds of being born here and having lived a great part of my life here. I am indeed East Anglian by birth. But why 'Modern'? Well I hope this will become clear as the reader reads on. He or she will learn that at several points in my working life I began to take less and less interest in my job as an educator and more and more interest in the work of my wife, Barbara, who, through her work ethic and ability, has become a renowned world figure in her profession. I am married to a person who began married life as a committed mother and housewife who, after ten years of marriage, trained for and eventually became a world renowned neuropsychologist. This required a revolution in our home, leading me to share the running of it, caring more for the children and becoming an assistant to Barbara when required. I have always enjoyed this partnership. It has led for instance to worldwide travels and abundant work as an editor and proof reader, and even a publisher. By the law of averages married couples will comprise in equal numbers of couples where the husband might be the more able or talented and sometimes the wife. But in the latter cases this is not always recognised. I came to realise that Barbara has greater talents than myself and we have continued our marriage in this knowledge. Thus, I might be justified in claiming 'modern man' status.

The quotation, "Better to find out than be told" was chosen by me because I like to think that I have tried to live my life in this way, certainly it was a guiding principle in my teaching. Originally, as far as I am concerned, the actual words were selected by readers to describe the government's Plowden Report into Primary education in England, and I'm not too sure whether they were chosen in praise or criticism. 'Plowden' was the unofficial name for the 1967 report for the Central Advisory Council for Education (England). The report is widely known for its praising of child centred approaches to education, stressing that at the 'heart of the education process was the child.' It was an increasingly liberal view of education stimulated by the relaxed attitude of people in the 1960's. It aimed to 'free schools constrained by the need to get good results.' It argued that IQ should not be regarded as infallible; that teachers should not assume that only what is measurable is valuable; and that teachers should help pupils to develop lively and enquiring minds.' Ever since the report's publication it seems to me that British politicians have been embarrassed by its recommendations and have ignored them in favour of more and more tests and examinations. I think, for example, of Michael Gove's disastrous abolition of course work as part of the GCSE Examination in the year 2012. As a result of my own research, I have come to recognise children need both to find out for themselves and sometimes they need gaps in their own learning and enquiry to be filled quickly and efficiently by a teacher who can save time by telling them. My sadness is that there is far too little of pupil centred enquiry and far too much giving of facts by teachers in many classrooms. In the sixties, the Americans called this kind of teaching 'the rule of two thirds: in any classroom, lecture hall or tutorial room the teacher talks for two thirds of the time, and for two thirds of that time facts are given.'

In the late 1980s I carried out a longitudinal study of children working in teacher-led and pupil-led discussion groups in order to compare what kinds of learning were going on and with what results. This research is described in later pages of this book.

I am conscious that much has been written in this book about Sarah, our eldest child, who died abroad in a white-water rafting accident. The last part of the book is devoted to a search for the site where she died and an account of our goodbye ceremony in the Cotahuasi valley in deepest Peru. Our other two children, Anna and Matthew, gave us no pain as they went through a comparatively straightforward childhood, school career, eventual work and partnerships. Our daughter, Anna, achieved success as a psychologist before committing to a more traditional role as a mother, grandmother and family leader; and Matthew became an internationally well known photographer attached to the wine industry concentrating on food, wine and travel. Matthew married Andrea, an internationally regarded wine maker. They live in Chile with their two boys, our grandsons Sammy and Max, who are bilingual, speaking both Spanish and English. Anna had a rocky marriage and gave birth to Rosie and Francesca before an eventual second highly rewarding marriage to Mike. She and Mike live near us in Bury St. Edmunds, Suffolk, her two children, Rosie and Francesca also live in Norfolk. Rosie has a daughter – our great granddaughter, Amélie, who is the treasure of the family and a total delight. She now lives with her new partner, Hope, who also has a child named Conroy; and Francesca is happily living with Jack. As I mentioned earlier, I was eventually able to take on quite a substantial role as a parent to our three children and during their early school years spent many daily hours with them while Barbara was completing a higher education which included a master's degree and Ph.D as well as professional preparation for her therapeutic work with brain injured people that led to many international honours, the publication of over thirty books and countless research papers as well as many famous lectureships around the world. In later years I accompanied Barbara on several international trips which were frequently followed by voyages of discovery in deserts, mountains and seas of the world. One of our favourite pursuits was African safaris and indeed Africa is Barbara's favourite continent having visited seventeen countries there. We know the USA and

Australasia very well having travelled extensively in both continents. It would be true to say that, in both of them Barbara's professional colleagues regard her as an honorary citizen. Barbara is indeed a world citizen having visited and worked in over one hundred countries.

The Story

Swinging outwards from the top of the wall he grasps the metal pole with both hands his feet flying outwards, round and round. The pole although bent from about six feet from the top holds fast as always when he does this. His hands burning, he levers himself back on to the wall before hurtling outwards again. There's just him and he knows it and enjoys it: it's his time alone, on his own, he doesn't need anyone. He's come along the barracks wall downhill to the bottom of his street, past the back of the shop that sells everything, along the top of a much thinner wall until he reaches this spot. He's the only one who does this and nobody sees him, and he thinks now that nobody will ever know.

It's 1943. The eight year old Ipswich boy is dressed in a floppy striped shirt and brown corduroy, knee length trousers belted with a snake clasp. The clothes are ill fitting, his boots are heavy and large, his knees are grazed. Although skinny he is athletic. Newson Street is on a hill, it forms a steep slope with terraced houses and their slated roofs running down one side and on the opposite side another wall about six feet high forming the backs of gardens that lead to a posher row of unterraced houses forming Orford Street. People in Orford Street don't want to know people in Newson Street. Except for his pal Adrian who is his best school mate and partner in football, cricket, swimming, cycling and fully accepted member of the Newson Street gang. This gang was formed at the beginning of the war and was run by two bigger boys. All had ranks from colonel through captain to lance corporal and private. Adrian and Mick were still privates but rapidly going through all the dangerous feats they had to conquer in order to climb the ranks. Mick had on the previous day passed the ringer test which involved a ruler being passed through the slim gap of two rollers (used formally for ringing out the water from rinsed piles of washing) and as a 'sergeant', Rex Stewart, turned the wheel gradually forcing the ruler deeper and deeper into Mick's stomach. In fact, the ruler broke and he hadn't had to shout at them to stop so he passed the test.

War time and all the dads had left home after being called up to join one of the services, so the boys had the streets to themselves. My dad was an exception as he was invalided out of the army with tuberculosis. Without fathers for the most part we were wild, untamed, out of mother's reach, thankfully for her and for them. The girls played their own games, mainly indoors or so it seemed; or else they were reading or helping sometimes in the home. Except in winter after there had been a fall of snow. Then the street was transformed with boys and girls taking part in sledging contests down the hill of the street which, at the bottom curved sharply to the right, almost at right angles. I think of how fast our sledge went, much faster than anybody else's. It was long and narrow and five people could sit on it comfortably as it raced towards the bottom and swept round the corner. Only very rarely there might have been a car coming round that corner but I can't remember it ever happening. It just added a slice more danger to think of a car coming the other way. Being war time Britain, hardly anyone had a car, not like today when you can't move freely in Newson Street because of cars parked all the way down the street.

The best night for snow was the time it began to fall at about five o' clock in the evening. It was a blinding blizzard. Incredible. And it didn't stop until about 9.00 p.m. As suddenly as it had started the snow stopped, the clouds disappeared, and a full moon shone down on the pure, clean street. The snow was above knee height for most of the kids. It was wonderful. No sledging in this deep snow but silence as everyone stood inside their doorways and regarded the transformed street, the bright round moon, its shine reflecting on the crystal roofs: stillness, contemplation, and wonder. Now eighty-six years old I have never seen such a dramatic fall of snow in such a short space of time: in England that is, as I *have* seen five feet of snow fall on a Colorado ranch in two days when I was in my late sixties. But that's another story. For now, I watch with my mother and sisters and know that it might be a couple of days before the snow becomes impacted and then, if it freezes, will provide the right conditions for an icy run downhill at speed with the sledge rumbling and the metal runners glistening, rushing to that corner which has to be negotiated with right foot digging into the ice to force the sledge round 90 degrees. The alternative would be to dive straight into a brick wall, not wanted.

Our house is just about in the middle of the street and is one of only six houses that has a passageway. This makes us a bit special I think as we have two ways of getting into the house whereas other residents can only enter from their front doors – unless of course they use the passageways and then walk round the backs of gardens by the barracks wall until they come to their own gateway if they have one. The passageway is cold in winter, cool in summer and always noisy with echoes when you walk along it. It has an uneven stone floor and the sides are formed by the red brick walls of the two next door houses. I can smell those bricks and stones to this day. We are a distinct community and in the Wilson's case we have a number of relations living in the same street. My nana and granddad Bennett live at number 62 as will my uncle Ray when he is demobbed after the war; my Irish grandma Wilson lives round the bottom corner at number 5, and we have a distant aunt and her two sons who live at number 60.

In 1943 I have two sisters one older than me and one younger; and we are soon to have another girl as my mum is pregnant. The oldest, Gloria, is considered, quite rightly, to be the beauty of the family. She is to go on to become Miss East of England in 1948, then a famous model at the Ipswich Art School, and a breaker of many hearts – including those of more than a few American servicemen who were stationed at Bentwaters camp. Gail is younger than me and is the nice one who is mum's right-hand helper in all housework, cleaning and cooking. I am just left alone to play in the gang and participate in all sports and teams and every kind of scrape possible. There are many of these, some extremely painful. Luckily for me I have always been able to run home to be comforted in a warm and welcoming nest by a mother who is archetypal in terms of the warmth, love and support she gives her children. My dad is always in the shadow and remains outside the protective warmth of us others. He works hard each day as a labourer at the manganese bronze company; he cycles to work before we get up and returns from work, tired and dirty, to eat his dinner before washing and going down to the pub to seek solace from his mates. Although my dad is not at all cruel to us, he remains an outsider in the home: he seemingly takes little notice of our schooling or our welfare. For example, later, when I was fifteen, I represented Ipswich schoolboys in a football match against a side from Germany. It was in 1951, one of the very first sporting meetings between Germans and British after the war. The Frankfurt boys were on a good will tour of the UK. Well, it took a lot of encouraging and persuading from mum to get my reluctant dad to this event. Can you imagine that today? Not keen to see your son play in an international game? Incidentally, the match ended in a 1-1 draw, and I had a poor game, stuck on the wing on what was a massive Portman Road pitch, hungry for a pass but not being allowed in those days to go looking for the ball. It was five forwards, three half backs and two backs system that did not encourage individuality or flair. My overriding memory of coaching in those days of leather boots and equally heavy balls was to *"Pass the ball!"* as soon as you got it!

How to describe our family circumstances? They were marked in the first place by poverty, which in our case was extreme, and then I would single out resourcefulness, which enabled us to get by quite successfully and lead lives that were for the most part happy and fulfilling. In this I am excluding my father who remained outside all that was happening in the household, home, neighbourhood, school and community. He had his own life and work from which we were, for the most part, unaware. Dad just could not cope with his family and so he led his own life at work and in the pub. He was never authoritarian or harsh towards us children, he just didn't seem to be part of the family. This situation was amplified by the fact that mum was Church of England and dad was Catholic. In fact, we children were christened as Catholics but attended the local St. Matthew's Church of England regularly for Sunday School and Sunday services. Neither church knew of this duality and I've often wondered whether hell would have been let loose if they did! We also attended the local St. Matthew's primary school. Dad was excluded from those areas where we were in community with others. The other fact was that mum and dad did not get along well and we children dreaded the rows that occurred between them almost on a daily basis. Looking back now I can appreciate my dad's position much more positively than I did at the time. He was almost an outcast in his own home and his social and family skills were so weak that he had no way of becoming part of the family apart from shouting at mum.

Mum loved us and loved life. She was an active *Young Mother* in the church, later to become a member of the *Mother's Union*. I was never sure when mothers moved from one to the other, at what age this was supposed to occur, but I was conscious of the fact that mum tried to delay joining the Mother's Union for quite some years. This delay was unwittingly encouraged by the Rector, Mr. Jones, who was an extremely handsome, dark Welsh man who was idolised by the women of the parish. I can't help thinking now of D.H. Lawrence's description of his mother and how she was encouraged by the vicar and his outlook to think beyond the confines of the small mining community to a wider world of culture, literature, and the arts. In her own small way this was what my mother was doing and it served her and us children very well later on when the first three of us passed the 11+exam and attended the grammar school.

In fact, what was remarkable about my mum was that she began to educate herself alongside her children as it were. Her reading increased and she began to go to the theatre and take some interest in art as her children's perspectives were extended in these areas through schooling. But I'm rushing ahead by too many years.

I mentioned resourcefulness as a counter to poverty earlier and this took many different forms. First, although mum was never able to buy us new clothes, she managed to keep us in regular stock by buying at jumble sales. She was an inveterate attendee at these functions and always managed to get to the front of any queue before doors opened. We were kitted out in some extraordinarily bizarre outfits at times but always managed to look impressive. At one time I remember my sister Carol, and this must have been in 1949 as she was then in the infant's class, came to school dressed in what can only be described as an Arabian pantomime costume with a tiny waistcoat, bare waist and flowing pantaloons. Her teacher was not as subtle as she thought she was when she sent Carol round to every class under the pretence of needing to inform every teacher about some made up message or other. I still remember my intense embarrassment as my teacher and the class looked on at my sister in astonishment!

At Christmas all our toys and other presents came from jumble sales, and I believe that my mother started her collection of these twelve months earlier. These Christmas items were kept at my nana's three doors away and then assembled in giant pillowcases on Christmas Eve. It never occurred to any of us to question the fact that these presents sometimes looked shop worn. It didn't matter to me that Father Christmas sometimes brought me toy soldiers with their paint worn off in places or their guns bent out of shape: they were presents at Christmas and they were as enchanting as the most luxurious item bought from the most expensive shop the day before.

Other ways of making extra money included assembling items such as garters that were to be sold in shops. All the family except dad entered into this activity. I think it may have been considered part of the war effort – although we never assembled shells or anything like that! Our favourite pastime involving the making of money was carol singing at Christmas time. My three sisters and I would approach this with considerable effort and expertise (unlike the carol singers of today who knock on one's door after a one-line "We wish you a Merry Christmas..." and expect to be given something for their efforts!). I was in the choir at St. Matthew's and my sisters were good singers anyway. We would practise for hours and then with lantern and song sheets would go out into the cold night to houses in Orford Street, Warrington Road, Paget Road, Constitution Hill, and other posh places and sing at least two full carols at each house. We got known for this and for a few years we were greeted by many residents with welcome smiles, hot mince pies and coins. We loved this and were proud to take our hoard back to mum who accepted the precious money in a somewhat Fagin-like manner. Mum was also 'good' as far as the black market was concerned. Her approach seemed to have been to get some butcher or baker or whoever to supply her with food beyond her rations and then use this act as some form of blackmail that meant that the purveyor, whoever he was, was hooked for the duration of the war and could not say no to little bits of extra now and then.

Reading was a passion for all of us. With no television we topped up our self-entertainment with a continuous supply of books from the public library, situated about a mile from our street. Sometimes I can remember we would each get five books out on a Friday, read them all before 4.00 p.m. on Saturday and rush back to the library to get another five books out so we'd have a supply in for Sunday. There was no one to advise us as to what to read so our approach remained uncritical. I for instance read through the complete volumes of "Bomba, The Jungle Boy" in the space of a few weeks, surely a series that has gone out of print today.

This extensive reading and constant talk at home broadened our education beyond that provided by St. Matthew's Primary School, which was attached to the church situated across the street. Here we learned how to spell, our tables by rote, handwriting, essay writing, arithmetic, geography (concentrating on the vast red bits of the world map that 'belonged' to us), history of the monarchs, nature study, and the Christian religion. We sat in rows, in double-desks that, in their shape and construction restricted our movements to little more than fidgeting. While it is true the teachers did not go in for pupil-led learning or many creative pursuits we did get a good grounding in the basics. This proved useful in the case of those who eventually passed the 11+ examination because that exam itself was not celebrated for encouraging children to learn creatively or *ask* questions. Much later, when I became a teacher in the 1960's, I was convinced that children learn by actively doing things, by talking together, asking questions, solving problems and finding answers. This was not on offer at St. Matthew's as we sat in our double desks in rows and listened to the one person allowed to talk in the classroom – the teacher. This sounds more critical than I want to be as – given the current orthodoxy at that time – our teachers were extremely hard working and encouraging in their own way. We did have fun at St. Matthew's and there were extra- curricular activities such as end of year drama and growing plants at the nature table. We also collected money for the war effort and I remember how Mr. Bonner, our head teacher, designed a series of targets in the shape of the RAF circles on aeroplanes, linked by a wire and strung out above our heads in the main hall. Each target had a sum of money printed on it and as this sum was surpassed a model spitfire attached to the wire would break through that particular target on its way to the end sum. We got there!

I remember very keenly a time in our last year at St. Matthew's when Mr. George our teacher got us to grow beans in jam jars. The jars contained blotting paper and we put water into the jars from time to time. It was a competition between several small groups of about four or five kids in each. There were two plants that were well ahead of the rest and one was ours, which grew tall and somewhat angular. The other was grown by a group of girls led by a tall and rather beautiful girl with lovely long hair. She was always immaculately dressed. Their plant was not as tall as ours but had fuller leaves. It was a neck and neck race and each day we would rush into the classroom to see which plant was growing ahead of the others. One morning as my group ran to see how our plant was doing, we were to see that its head was curled downwards and its angular stem was turning black. It was dead! I suppose I suffered my first bout of grief at the dreadful loss. Later that day – at break – we had a chance to examine our plant closely and discovered a vertical cut in its stem about halfway up. Just the kind of insertion that could be made by a thumb nail if your nails were quite long. Despite our protests and wails of disbelief and shock Mr. George did not pursue the matter. However, I can remember the long haired, immaculate girl observing us silently and it was not long before I put two and two together after noticing her long, well-manicured nails. Nothing was ever proven; her group went on to win the competition and my grief was fuelled by a sense of injustice. Maybe a good preparation for adult life?

We had much fun at school when the air raid warning sounded, signalling enemy planes above and an orderly march, in classes, each child with a gas mask, to the long air raid shelter that was dug deep beneath a near-by field and accommodated the whole school. None of us was ever frightened. Rather, we regarded the war and the occasional bombings as a huge adventure. Down in the shelter we sang songs at the tops of our voices: "This old man he played one, he played nick knack on my drum..."

Because of physical restriction in the classroom we did tend to go a little crazy in the playground. The school had two of these: one was asphalt and surrounded by a tall wooden fence, this was for the infants; and the other, for seniors, was a large circular space set amongst numerous gravestones forming the graveyard that surrounded the church. We were never aware of how macabre this might appear to others as we played our games of German and British among the graves. We usually split into these two nations and fought air battles throughout play time. I was always the German Squadron Leader and felt more than a tinge of pride at cutting such a dashing and exotic figure. Our battles took the form of boys running around the playground imagining they were aeroplanes. Our arms held out wide, we would make howling sounds for the engines and spluttering noises for machine guns as we mimicked spitfires and Messerschmitt's hounding each other in the skies.

One day we were playing in this manner when one of the boys noticed a figure lying on top of the stone top of one of the raised graves. As we approached the grave with some trepidation we were amazed and frightened to see a large, black man. Was he dead or asleep? This was in fact the first black person most of us had ever seen. We were certainly not a part of a multicultural society in those days, hence the bewilderment we all felt as we rushed into school to tell our teachers. The man turned out to be a drunken American airman who was sleeping off a heavy night he'd had in one of the Ipswich pubs. The American airmen were to become a welcome sight in Ipswich during the war even though it was always puzzling to us kids that the blacks and their white counterparts were always separated into two groups each having their own pubs to frequent. I remember that the military police always travelled one white and one black in order to deal with occasional outbreaks of fighting and drunkenness.

It seemed that black people were welcomed much more into Ipswich society than they ever were in their own squadrons. Later on, transport was provided for young Ipswich women to be bussed out to American bases in Lakenheath, Mildenhall and Bentwaters for weekend dances and so forth. My sister Gloria was one of them and to my delight she befriended a most impressive young black man who was a 'Golden Gloves' champion boxer. Previously I had been even more impressed with Al because he was a genuine Apache Indian. In fact, he came to stay with us at Christmas. He was such an exotic figure for me to boast about at school! He was one of the camp's bouncers, an extremely tough looking, huge man who looked like Jack Palance. I remember he used to lift my mum into his jeep - and she must have weighed about eighteen stones in those days! Much to my disappointment in later years Gloria married an Englishman who was a journalist for the Ipswich Evening Star. Poor David has never managed to live up to my early expectations of an Apache or black boxer brother-in-law!

The cinema was a huge part of our lives, as it was for everybody in those days. Saturday morning pictures, held in the town's two biggest cinemas, the Regent and the Odeon, were attended by masses of children. Besides the black and white films of Tarzan, starring Johnny Weissmuller, the cowboy films starring Roy Rogers, comedies, starring Bud Abbot and Lou Costello etc., there were competitions and sing alongs to the electric organ that would rise from the depths in all its glory while a brightly suited, sleek haired man would roll out the tunes. Many of the kids had chewing gum that they had begged from American servicemen.

"Got any gum chum?" was the expression we always used and frequently we were rewarded by kindly Americans, many of them no doubt missing their own sons and daughters far away in Hollywood Land.

My mother used to take us to the pictures and much to our extreme embarrassment she would at times when she had no money, take us in the 'back way'. Many a time we hung round the back door of a cinema with other scraggy kids and the one lone mother, waiting for the back exit to be opened at which point we all rushed in. Once we were stopped by an usherette who shone her torch on my mother and us three kids, but mum just walked imperiously to a set of four spare seats and sat us down. The usherette hadn't the nerve to challenge mum. My God! The agonies I went through on those occasions...

There were at times many British troops stationed in Ipswich, presumably before they were shipped off to various parts of the world to fight. We were lucky enough to have about twenty of them living in the big house in Anglesea Road just at the top of Newson Street. We loved visiting the soldiers and they seemed to enjoy us being there. They would joke and josh with us and sometimes let us hold their rifles or bren guns. Of course, this thrilled us enormously. Our lives were very exciting, and the war was a big adventure for us. We may have been hungry at times, unwashed and badly clothed, but we were never bored and never bothered mum. Even the occasional bombing held adventure rather than terror. Only once did we ever get to our air raid shelter in the black-out down the bottom of the garden, preferring to stay under the stairs where it was warmer. Unlike some of our neighbours, men too old to be called up, who had built their shelters into comfortable places where a family could eat and sleep in comfort and warmth, our shelter was always cold, comfortless and damp – so much so that when we rushed in on that one occasion we were up to our ankles in cold water! Another thing I remember is that our dad had laid the small plot of land in front of the air raid shelter to lawn and had covered the newly seeded ground with pegs and black cotton to keep the birds off. Well, when we rushed to the shelter that night, with the air raid warning sounding in our ears we trampled the cotton and pegs and newly sown seed into a desolate, unrecoverable tangle! Dad was in his element during the air raids and would stand in the garden looking up at the sky hoping to see German bombers caught in the arc of search lights. I don't think this ever happened.

One incredible memory I have is of a spitfire chasing a German aeroplane across the sky. I was in the garden standing on top of the air raid shelter and looking southwards over towards a park when this German plane came out from the west followed by the spitfire. I could see fiery red streaks coming from the spitfire's wings and striking the German plane, which had black smoke coming from its tail. The German plane started to spiral down and out of view. The next thing I could see was a parachute high, high up in the sky. It seemed to be much higher than the planes but couldn't have been. The parachutist drifted towards the east and out of sight. Next day I learned that the German pilot had landed near a factory known as Cranes. He was soon surrounded by workers from the factory. When the police arrived, the German pilot had lost his belongings including his watch so it was said. This was to be my one and only direct sight of the second world war in action. To this day I can see that action as clearly as if it was happening before me. It was not a memory of a film I had seen because all those films were in black and white, and this was in colour.

I mentioned that my nana and granddad Bennett lived at number 62 Newson Street. While granddad was there as a smiling, friendly soul who greeted us cheerily on his return from work, it was nana who I remember most clearly as she went out of her way to help my mum and us children cope with the demands of daily living and sustenance. Nana was a small, thin woman, a bundle of nerves with a mind full of anxieties and fears. She was never known to walk anywhere, always running whether it was round her small house or down Newson Street or on her way to town. She ran to the shops, she ran down the street, she ran round her home, she rarely sat still. She was also, I think now, terribly afraid of crossing any kind of authority and I believe her condition was possibly some form of innate paranoia. Her most helpful contribution to our well-being was in her preparation of toast for us kids each morning. When we got downstairs, we were greeted by the lovely smell of toast prepared on a coal fire and we would see a huge bundle of thinly cut (before the time of sliced bread) soft buttered toast waiting for us in the hearth. She did this for us each morning throughout our schooling.

Nana was constantly worrying in case she had done something wrong. Later on, her anxieties caused her to suffer from extreme eczema, most of her body covered in a thick layer of red and sore wounded skin. Each day our granddad had to bathe her in oils and bandage her arms and legs. I need to digress here and bring the reader up to date because what I must report relates most directly to nana and her ancestors. I have recently been able to call on the services of a young man who has been able to trace nana's genealogy back to an ancestor who was born in 1569. The reason why we have been able to go back so far is partly because the family almost never strayed from their close-knit lives in a Suffolk village and its immediate surroundings. These ancestors were in the main labourers and peasants who worked on the farms or in a local fur and skin factory in the village. They were always poor to the extent of being destitute at times and they seem always to have been dominated by parson, landowner and police force. In the early nineteenth century for example, there are records from local newspapers reporting on various petty crimes and misdemeanours committed by my ancestors. They stole partridge eggs and ducks from the landowner's property, trespassed on land for the purpose of finding animals and vegetables to eat, they got drunk and disorderly at times. It seems to me when reading these reports that perhaps my ancestors were, in their anti- establishment way, fighting almost heroically against a society that placed an impossibly heavy lid on working class aspirations and their desperate need to survive. There was no way up, no way to better oneself, no way to find enough to eat - except to make a stand through minor crimes. My hero amongst them has to be Adam, who is first reported as facing execution for having stolen a sheep. He and fourteen other men, guilty of other crimes, were sentenced to be hanged in 1820. Their sentence was at the last moment suspended and they were sent to a hulk in Portsmouth and eventually shipped out to Australia. I later learned that Adam completed his sentence and received a pardon 40 or so years later, returned to

Suffolk and died there. The reports on my ancestors continued when several of them were either killed or wounded in the First World War. They suffered for, were punished by, and even died for an authoritarian establishment, a hierarchy that didn't give a damn for their well-being. Happily, the family record ends with what I think is the most positive sign when the local paper describes the first Union meeting to be held in the village. Amongst those attending were Peter and Tom. Perhaps this would be the start for them of new ways of regarding society, education, proper payment for work and an end to the spurious but excessively damaging rule by others who got their authority through privilege not merit?

The landscape in which we spent our war time childhood seems on reflection to have been almost idyllic. Once you had walked to the top of Newson Street and turned right along Anglesea Road you came to Henley Road with its entry into a quite magnificent arboretum with its wonderful borders and beds of flowers kept meticulously by the gardeners. My mother took us to this manicured fairy land on many occasions where we would have our picnic of jam sandwiches and free orange juice provided by the public services. This orange juice will be remembered by all children of the forties as the best they have ever tasted. It came in squarish bottles and was quite thick but when water was added it tasted of true oranges. Having written this I am left wondering whether we didn't get this orange juice until the fifties when Labour was in power? Also, I don't think many oranges were seen in the UK during the actual war when German submarines were on the prowl. Another thing I remember vividly about the arboretum was the succession of couples that met there for somewhat restricted but nevertheless seemingly exciting and passionate embraces. These couples were always made up of either American or British servicemen and the local women and, I imagine now, possibly some desperate housewives. The song the Americans brought with them, "Roll me over in the clover..." was very apt for what we kids said we saw from a distance.

From the arboretum you could walk through a gate and into the magnificent Christchurch Park where we spent most of our leisure hours. We played cricket endlessly in summer and football in winter. We were hardly ever at home. I can remember on Saturdays I'd play football in the special league for local boy scouts in the mornings and then after lunch go up the park to play more football until dusk when the park wardens, known as 'parkies' would blow their whistles to chase us out of the gates. When I was older the scout league was replaced by various school teams of rugby, hockey and cricket, but I still ended up in Christchurch Park kicking or batting a ball around with my mates. In winter when there had been snow we made use of the one big hill in Ipswich that was in the centre of Christchurch Park and along with hundreds of other adults and children from Ipswich we would spend hours pulling our sledges uphill and then fly downhill at what seemed like incredible speeds. Again, our wooden, narrow sledge seemed to be one of the fastest machines there.

When you turned left at the top of Newson Street you would follow Anglesea Road until you came to Paget Road, which, if you turned right came to the bottom of Valley Road. This would take about fifteen minutes. By this time, you had arrived at another wonderland consisting of Broomhill Park with its large open air swimming pool where we played, sunbathed and swam all day long. Almost next to the pool was a magical place we kids called the 'undergrowth'. It was truly that and consisted of a very large crater like indentation filled with dark undergrowth and strangely misshapen trees. There was a pond right in the middle where tadpoles, frogs and newts lived happily until disturbed by robber boys and girls. We loved this place, our own jungle that seemed on reflection to be similar to the Hollywood version inhabited by Johnny Weissmuller (Tarzan), his rescued girlfriend Jane and their pet chimpanzee that we saw on our screens on Saturday mornings. We were lean because of rationing anyway, we walked or cycled everywhere, and we swam in and ran around that swimming pool for hours on end. Later on, I began to notice older girls, some of whom were deeply tanned and therefore exotic. One of the most beautiful of these was particularly breath taking in her allure and graceful movements but of course she was out of our reach as she talked only to a succession of older men who were her admirers and companions. She seemed to us to be like one of the unobtainable screen stars we could only look upon and not touch. Several years later, as a young man who played trumpet in the Ipswich Jazz Band during the New Orleans revival of the mid fifties I got to know this young woman, who had become one of the stars of the Ipswich Art School and frequented the jazz scene.

As I'm writing this, I ask myself what is my earliest memory and for this I have to go back before 1939, when I was four years old. I had been given a birthday present of a toy gun with wooden handle and tin barrel. It had a cork attached to the barrel by a piece of string and you stuck the cork into the mouth of the barrel, fired the gun and the cork flew out as far as the string would allow it. I was in Christchurch Park I was dressed in a light green coat and matching hat, and I was obviously in love with my gun. I was walking near the round pond with iron railings round its circumference when an older boy came up to me, snatched the gun from me and threw it far into the middle of the pond. I was devastated, sobbing and inconsolable. The gun was lost for good.

My cousin Cedric was a great friend. He lived in Anglesea Road in one of the posh council houses. He was always playing football in Newson Street with me. He was in the same class as me and always seemed to be brighter and harder working. He was very nervous though and because of this he let himself down in the 11+ exam and failed it while I passed. What a mockery! Cedric had to go to the tough local secondary modern boy's school when he would have flourished at the grammar. He would have loved an academic life and he would have knuckled down to the disciplines easily. Cedric became a bank manager in adulthood.

We two used to go fishing for carp in a somewhat mucky pond somewhere in the country about five miles from home. One day we decided to bring one of the carp we caught home with us – in a large jar. We didn't know what to do with it until I remembered that the two old ladies who lived at number 60 had a long tin bath in their garden, used as a water butt. We put the fish in there and secretly fed it each day with bread. Nobody found out but I can't remember what happened to the fish. The two old ladies always dressed in long black dresses and wore black bonnet hats, looking like ladies from the Victorian era. One day I was chasing round the end of Newson Street and into Orford Street when one of the old ladies was coming in the opposite direction. There was a crash and the old lady fell to the ground and as she did so her hat fell off – and so did her wig to reveal a completely bald head! I was petrified and thought I might have killed her. I just ran away. A few days later I saw her walking in the street, still alive.

I'm not sure whether the war had anything to do with the fact that boys used to fight a lot at school and in the streets. I have to own up that I was among the guiltiest and for quite some time, way into the fourth or fifth year at grammar school, I built a reputation for being a fighter. There was never the violence we see today with the use of knives or any other kind of weapons. The fights were always with fists and tended to follow the Queensbury rules. There was never any bullying but lots of challenges at which point a ring of shouting boys would gather and urge the two boys involved to 'fight, fight, fight.' When I say there was no bullying, I mean this code existed among the fighters. I did see bullying and I was always sickened by it and to this day I can remember with horror a boy who happened to be fat when he was about thirteen to fourteen years old being called 'fat arse' by a group of boys. He was absolutely desperate in his attempts to catch the chanting mob, flustered and wretched, he ran round and round but could not catch them. Later on, he and I became best friends – in the sixth form. He, the academic, studious scholar and me, captain of rugby etc., all round sportsman and struggling student. Our friendship was bonded in our shared love of early New Orleans jazz.

There were occasions when I, myself, was bullied by older boys. This was when we were still at primary school. I can remember, for instance, being stripped to my underpants and thrown into a trench of stinging nettles. Once we were chased by another group of older boys armed with catapults. They caught us and lined us up against a large wooden wall of some building or other and then fired stones from their catapults so that they kept just missing us. It was terrifying our eyes tightly shut and hearing those stones crash into the wood and wondering if we were going to be hit.

My inevitable come uppance as far as fighting is concerned - and I want to get this shameful violent aspect of my childhood done and dusted before returning to other happier memories of my life in the years before the end of the war – was at the hands or rather fists, teeth and boots of Walter Staff. Walter was a tall, gangly, blonde lad of fifteen and as far as I know had never been in a fight at school. We had a row one day and decided to settle it after school behind the bicycle racks. A crowd gathered and the fight began, me trying to box cleverly but Walter seemingly not wanting to know the rules laid into me with feet, fists, and nails. We were soon flailing across bicycles in the racks, first one way then the other. Then Walter had my hair in his hands and was pushing my face into a concrete post. I lost a shoe and was still trying to box, looking quite ridiculous when Walter landed into me again. I was knocked to the floor and was bleeding from cuts to my face. We could go on, but I knew I was beaten. Walter stood there before me, this young lad who had never had a fight before and I lamely asked that I might put my shoe back on. This broke the spell and, even more lamely, I pointed out that I had to get to my paper round. It was over – apart from some triumphant jeering from a few boys who were enjoying my downfall. And that was that: I never fought at school again and only had one other fight in my life - when I was attacked by three soldiers outside Woolwich Barracks during National Service.

My gentle cousin Cedric used to come round to Newson Street where we played football, table tennis in my granddad and nana's house, or participated in the Newson Street gangs semi-military activities – which included preparing for any attacks from the Geneva Road council estate gang. For example, I can remember, covering the tops of steep walls between the top two houses in the street with broken, jagged glass, which we were going to push down upon the heads of our rivals during any attack. When the attack did come it simply took the form of a face-off with scores of them standing at the top of our street while our pathetic, hungry-looking, scruffy dozen or so grouped half way down the street. The two groups just stared at each other, no-one daring to make the first move until one of us threw a stone that hit one of their lads who gave out a yell of anguish. Then they rushed us. We simply ran into our houses and that was that. We won!

As I suggested before, the local church played a very important part in our young lives, not so much from a religious point of view but rather from a communal one. I have spoken of my mother's interest in the Young Wives and Mother's Union. It is true to say that, because most of the eligible men and husbands were absent at war, the vicar had it all to himself. He was extremely good looking, athletic, always sun tanned and had the most perfect voice with its lilting Welsh accent. My dad, in his Catholic distance from us all, hadn't a chance! My sisters threw themselves into the various clubs organised by the C.of E. church and always figured strongly in any dramatics, choirs, or dances. As a choir boy I attended church twice each Sunday and like most of them I fiddled underneath the camouflage of my cassock while looking beatific and innocent. Have you ever wondered why choir boys look so carried away?

The choir always had an annual occasion which took the form of a great party in the church hall in Clarkson Street. The idea was that each mum would make a special dish so there was an element of competition which led to a splendid feast. One year I remember my mum grumbling about this as she had hardly anything in the larder and was not the greatest of cooks anyway. She hit on the idea of collecting some elderberries which were in fruit at that time and making a trifle. Well, my sister and I watched her prepare this trifle and to our dismay she didn't even take the fruit off the skinny tangle of twigs; she just threw them into a bowl, twigs and all and poured a very thick custard over them. It set quickly and to this day I can see that trifle looking quite appetising and with just the tiniest thumb mark on its surface slightly reducing its aesthetic effect. However, at the party we were all sitting round a T shaped set of tables with the vicar's wife sitting in the centre of the top table – at which was placed my mum's trifle amongst other dishes. I had previously told the choir boys not to choose the trifle so of course it held their attention. Their looks were accompanied by quite a lot of sniggering and whispering "Don't eat the yellow trifle. Mick's mum made it." When it came to dessert time the vicar's wife had first choice and to my horror and the other boys' suppressed amusement, she looked at mum's trifle and said, "I'd like some of that." A server began to scoop a spoonful out of the dish and as she did so the elderberry twigs rose to the surface in a runny mess. The vicar's wife cried out, "That's enough!" and her dish was set before her. Nobody else chose that dish and the poor vicar's wife made one attempt to eat a spoonful and left the rest.

Many, many years later, when I was in my fifties I think, I saw the film 'Deliverance' in which a group of men go on a fishing trip which ends up with them killing a ghastly man who was a member of a gang who had tried to kill them. The man's body was tied up and weighted down and thrown into the river and the group of men make their way home thinking that was the end of their horrible adventure. However, as the film credits etc. appear on the screen, in the background the audience can see the river and they watch in horror as the dead man's bound hand and fingers come to the surface, making the silent point that, although the film had ended, the men's troubles were in no way over. When I saw that man's hand I was reminded of my mum's trifle, the way the elderberry twigs rose to the surface once the spoon had broken the surface.

The end of war

What celebrations! I was 10 years old and I made my way down to the centre of town, to an area known as "Electric House", which was a large open square bordered by Tower Ramparts Secondary Modern School for Boys, the Electric House itself, a large pub and various other buildings. It was also the main stopping area for corporation buses. Tonight there was a stage, an American band and crowds of joyful people out to have the best time of their lives. There were British and American sailors, airmen and soldiers, civilians and loads of young women. Everybody was dancing, crazily jitterbugging and embracing. One scene was extraordinarily puzzling to me. Two American servicemen had dressed as women and were dancing together very affectionately. I *could not* work this out. What was going on? I had a lot of growing up to do before I realised that on that one-day taboos could be broken and no-one would object or turn violent or imprison people with non-mainstream sexual mores! Sadly, it was to be many further years, even decades before people with alternative sex lives could come out and be accepted by society. In the meantime, racism and homophobia were dark clouds obscuring understanding and acceptance. In the 1950s I heard of incidents of brutality and witch hunts that were utterly loathsome! They were not always "the good old days" that nostalgia fools us into believing.

But this was victory and everybody was intoxicated by thoughts of freedom and peace. All of us kids were looking forward to street parties, and if my mum had anything to do with it, the Newson Street party was going to be the best. It was. I don't need to go into details because everyone is familiar with what went on. The unique extra that my mum organised was a visit from two of the performers who were currently working at the Ipswich Hippodrome. These were the legendary Elsie and Doris Waters, known as Gert and Daisy in film and on radio. My mum had gone to the Hippodrome and backstage she barged into their dressing room and invited them to the Newson Street VE Party. Yes, of course they would be delighted to attend! The picture I have in my mind is of Gert and Daisy, perfectly well dressed and with close fitting hats talking their dry patter to the amusement of the adults in the street. As far as I know, nobody had a camera in Newson Street to record this sensational event! A little bit of research shows that Gert and Daisy are particularly remembered for their contribution to film and radio entertainment during World War II. They were stalwarts of the BBC radio variety programme "Workers' Playtime", where they would talk about anything and everything, but especially about their fictional husbands Bert and Wally. The two sisters were awarded OBEs in 1946. One other thing I learned is that Manchester United's defenders Gary Pallister and Steve Bruce were nicknamed Gert and Daisy by their fans in the late 90's!

So the war was over and I had another year to go before passing the 11+ exam enabling me to go to Grammar School. I remember my uncle Ray coming home from the Far East where he had been a wireless operator on board a sea plane. He stayed with his parents, my grandad and nana at 62 Newson Street. Ray was very handsome and liked to play the returning hero. We idolised him and would do anything for him. Cedric and I continued our games of street football, played with a tennis ball, but now we had an expert who watched us. We played for Ray and one day when Cedric beat me I was devastated and I think I may even have cried. Beaten in front of Uncle Ray! He took pity on me and allowed me to make him tea, collect coals from the back yard and stoke the fire for his comfort. I forgot my woes in being this close to him. He was an outstanding local footballer and was recognised as a heart throb in Ipswich. One day when the local Ransome and Rapiers Company had their Christmas party to which all the kids were invited

Uncle Ray went on stage to sing a popular song of the day: "I don't want to set the world on fire/I just want to put a flame in your heart". As with all things Ray was a good crooner. My sisters and I were captivated – as was the whole audience!

Something was in the air those days politically and although I was too young to appreciate any subtleties I did get caught up in the atmosphere and excitement of politics at the soapbox level. My mother was passionately involved and used to attend every meeting held at the Ipswich Baths Hall or Corn Exchange. I went with her sometimes and I remember her being amongst a very small minority of women. Mostly the halls were filled with men...and smoke. On one occasion my mother took my baby sister Carol, and I was terribly embarrassed when she breast fed Carol in front of those men! I think it was almost unheard of in those prudish days, but my mum was my mum and she, in this instance, was years ahead of her times. Like everybody else in Newson Street, we were all Labour supporters, and my special memory was of Clement Attlee coming to speak at the Corn Exchange at the 1945 election. He was so quiet and almost self-effacing but nevertheless a remarkable orator. At one point a black cat crossed under his feet – much to the amusement of the audience and it was years later that I realised that this was a plant to signify good luck. On the night of the General Election mum took us all to the cinema to see "The Rocking Horse Winner" a film based on a story by D.H. Lawrence. The idea was to spend time being entertained so that we could stay up as the results started to come in on the radio round about midnight. We stayed up till three in the morning by which time it was clear that Labour had won a landslide victory. By this time everybody in Newson Street was standing on their doorsteps sharing in the sense of victory and anticipation that things were going to be different from now on. The future held nothing but promise for us. Socialism would at last bring greater equality: putting an end to the hateful downstairs-upstairs society my parents had been brought up in; putting an end to education that favoured only the rich and powerful; putting an end to officers and men, putting an end to war; putting an end to poverty; putting an end to the divisions between those who lived in Paget Road and those of us who lived in Newson Street. Well...we would see.

The late forties

These years were strange ones for me, and I find them the hardest to recall. I went to grammar school in 1946 and for five years I wasted my time there. I cannot recall doing any homework, I remember being always tired and sleepy in class and consequently not attending to the teachers. My parents were no help at all, and I cannot, for instance, recall any time when they urged me to take studies seriously. It wasn't their fault as they were not equipped to deal with educational concerns. I had passed the 11+ and that was all that mattered to them. I was also taken ill mentally in my twelfth year and had some kind of breakdown. It developed as a fear that I would commit some crime when I grew up. I thought everybody knew this secretly and for a long time I thought everybody was watching me. It got so bad that my mother took me to the children's clinic where a doctor prescribed calcium powder and because I was extremely thin at that time, I had to have malt extract twice a day at school. There were two of us who took this revolting tasting stuff and we had to do it publicly in front of all the other boys. I was painfully skinny, and I don't know why. I was at the same time very athletic and starred at football after school and rugby on the school playing field. I was an all-rounder, gaining medals for swimming and lifesaving, representing my school house in all team games and later I was to win the school cross country. My skinniness disappeared as I approached later school years and I began to develop an athletic body through exercises and weightlifting that I learned from my time in the Boy Scouts. I was always a tremendous eater and have remained so throughout my life. At college for instance there was always a group of about five or six of us who deliberately stayed behind to have seconds of everything once all the other students had left the dining hall.

My nervous breakdown disappeared and I remain convinced that it all started from reading the grotesque rubbish that was printed in the gutter press. To this day I remain appalled by the stuff that gets printed in certain newspapers. In my late teens I fought my parents tooth and nail over their reading of these newspapers and my adult political beliefs have strengthened my view that the working class are frequently rendered apathetic by a British press that drugs them with tales of misdemeanours by celebrities and tales of murder, scandal and violence. In the middle of my early troubles, I was convinced I was going to grow up to be a murderer and I used to cry myself to sleep every night at the thought of this. Perhaps the calcium worked! Anyway, I grew out of my fears and was able to lead a normal but lazy schoolboy's life from then on.

Before I go on with my life in the late forties, I want to highlight some brief moments when my dad participated in family life. On Sundays for instance, he always came home from the pub at lunchtime to eat the Sunday lunch that had been kept warm for him in the oven. In his alcoholic merriment - despite my mother's wrath at his wasted hours drinking - he would become very generous and would give us half crowns. He showed his fondness for us at those times, and I now look back with disappointment that those moments that felt like love were so brief. I also remember a time when he came to a school open day and a cricket match was organised between the school and the fathers. I was so proud of my dad because he was the only father who actually ran out to the wicket to bat. I can see him doing this to this day. I can also see him running back after being out for a duck. But that didn't matter. He looked good did my dad. He was extremely handsome and quite dashing. There was also a time when he came to Broom Hill swimming pool with all of us. My mum didn't swim but he came in the pool and actually climbed to the top board in order to dive in. This was in our eyes an exceptional feat. Only the really brave could tackle that height! I remember my two sisters and I sitting at the side with my mother for what seemed ages before he dived, and we all laughed so heartily as he disappeared somewhat frog-like with legs apart into the deep end.

My dad loved reading cowboy books and I think he regarded himself as one of those silent, brave types as he read in bed with a fag burning in his mouth: another picture of him I can bring to mind readily. A very special occasion was the birth of my sister Carol in 1942. On the night she was due it was my dad's annual work's dinner and dance, held at the quite posh Crown and Anchor Hotel. He was taking my two sisters and me to this event and it was agreed that should the baby be born while we were there a message would be delivered to the Crown and Anchor and an announcement made publicly. This actually happened! At the end of one dance an official looking man got up on stage and announced to great cheers that Tom Wilson had just become a father for a fourth time. That was it for us. We all tore out of the hall, grabbed our coats, and ran all the way home in the dark, past Barrack Corner, along Norwich Road, up Orford Street and into Newson Street. We crashed through the front door and up to the middle bedroom where mum was lying awake and our new baby, Carol, safely tucked up in the open top drawer of a chest of drawers.

Around this time there is a photograph of my cousin Cedric and me standing with my granddad in his back garden at number 62. We must have been eleven years old, and we are dressed in boy scouts' uniform. I am looking very thin and knobbly kneed, and Cedric looks much better fed. We loved the boy scouts, and our particular troop was the seventh. We were a privileged troop in that we had a relationship with Lord Belstead which enabled us to go on weekend camps on his land. So many happy times there: we learned about different knots, how to establish a camp, make a kitchen, cook basic foods, erect great heavy tents, follow tracks of different animals and birds and so on. Scouting in Ipswich at that time was very strong, there were many troops from all different neighbourhoods. On Saturday mornings we took part in the scout football league and as I said before we then went on to play in school teams in the afternoons and might end our Saturdays with a kick around in Christchurch Park. We were always on the move and as fit as fiddles. We walked or cycled everywhere, and there was of course no television. I remember Cedric and I spent one whole day searching for cars, the idea being that he would tick off every time he saw an Austin seven and I would do the same for Morris tens. At the start of the day we bet each other that our particular car was in the ascendancy as far as numbers were concerned. We started out early with our packs of jam sandwiches and orange juice and spent the whole day roaming the streets of Ipswich looking for these cars and ticking them off. I am sad to report that Cedric won quite easily.

On one occasion the Ipswich scouts held a great competition in which each troop provided a representative patrol which would go round Ipswich to various points where they would be judged on their skills at knots, first aid, tracking, highway code etc. I was patrol leader and we cycled to these different locations around Ipswich. Disaster was not quite avoided when we turned up at the station for highway code, situated near the Regent cinema. We had our floppy hats on and carried our lengthy and somewhat heavy staves which made cycling difficult. As we approached the examiner at the Regent Cinema station I tried to salute him with one hand while holding on to my stave in a horizontal position along the frame of the bike. Unfortunately this led to a near garrotting of the examiner and me trying desperately to control a wobbling bike whilst saluting. My patrol members never forgave me for this awful start to our highway code examination!

My scouting days ended abruptly. After the annual scout swimming competition, in which I featured strongly being fast at front crawl, I was called to a special meeting at the previous scout leader's house. He was in there waiting for me with our new scout leader, a tightly arranged man who I thought looked better suited to the Hitler youth than the boy scouts. We didn't get on too well and I wondered what was coming. The new leader accused me of bullying my patrol at a Whitsun weekend camp at Belstead Brook at which incidentally our patrol won the competition for being the best organised. I was shocked as I thought I had been a very fair leader, but the new man insisted that I should be expelled from the troop. I knew deep down that he regarded me as insubordinate because of our mutual dislike. However, there was nothing I could do about it: I was expelled there and then. I was dismayed and felt particularly cheated as the troop had used me that same night to win races for them in the swimming competition. Only a few weeks later there was a scandal when the new leader was arrested for 'interfering with young children'. I did not return to the Seventh Ipswich Troop.

Wilson family in the forties

There's another photograph, this time of the whole Wilson family taken in our back garden at number 56. This must have been taken in 1948 when I was thirteen years old at which age, I was filling out and had lost the 'Belsen' look that certain boys used to refer to. My mother features as the main character and fills the middle space, my oldest sister Gloria, aged fifteen, is standing to the left and I am on the right; my sisters Gail, aged ten, and Carol, aged four, are sitting in front, and my dad is a shadowy figure at the back. The photograph tells its own story supporting observations I have made earlier that mum dominated with her outgoing, positive nature and dad seems to have positioned himself as though he is tagged on to the family unit rather than an essential part of it. Forty five years later I returned to that scene having walked through the stone passage. I was staggered to find that the wooden fence behind us in the photograph was still there!

I supported Ipswich Town when they were in the Third Division South and along with Adrian Bradbeer, we would go to the Portman Road ground sometimes on a Saturday afternoon. One day that sticks in my mind was round about the time that the film "The Third Man" was being shown, so this must have been as late as 1951. The music for the film was played on a zither and it became a top hit. Before the players came on to the field some of the current top ten hit records would be played and I can remember Adrian and I standing in the Churchmen's Road end of the ground and being thrilled by this wonderful zither music before the game. The film itself I still maintain is the best British film ever made. I have seen it many times and recently I was lucky enough to do the Third Man walk round Vienna when our enthusiastic guide took us to many of the parts of Vienna that were shot for the film. We finished our tour at the famous doorstep where Orson Welles was spotted by the light of some open casements and as the cat rubbed itself on his shoes. The spine-tingling effect for us on the tour was made even more pleasurable by the fact that a student was playing the Third Man theme on a zither for us! Just round the corner from the doorway.

I can still remember some of the more famous Ipswich players including Jennings who once scored a spectacular goal from outside the penalty area when he had his back turned to the goal mouth. I also remember one of the most popular players by the name of Brown, who had a special trick whereby the ball seemed to have been lost behind him so that the tackling back stopped in his tracks only to lose the ball which was then dragged forward by Brown's trailing foot. I once saw Brown on a bus a few years after his playing days were over and I was struck by how small and insignificant he was with a cherry faced drinker's face.

I mentioned earlier that my sister Gloria became Beauty Queen for Ipswich, and this was when I was in the second year at Northgate School so I was twelve or thirteen years old. I was terribly embarrassed to go to school the day after the story was published in the local Evening Star and the East Anglian Daily times. My school mates ragged me and the news got into the school staff room. I felt humiliated and I don't know why. Was I even at that age aware of the silliness of beauty contests? It got worse when Gloria was crowned Miss East England and with three other contestants competed for the ultimate prize of being Miss England, shown on Pathe News at all cinemas. Thankfully Gloria did not win that contest and instead concentrated on her duties as Miss East England by attending local fetes and carnival processions, being carted round the streets of Ipswich and other places much to my horror.

At school I continued to do disastrously, no homework ever completed, falling into a hazy sleep in the classroom, and getting a record number of detentions for insolence. What a disaster I was and what a waste of everybody's time, especially mine! The tiredness may have been caused by the fact that I had to get up at 5.30 a.m. every morning to make my way to a newsagent's shop where I wrote out the paper rounds for other boys who turned up at 7.00 a.m. to go on their rounds. I did this throughout my school career, earning 10 shillings a week pocket money. Mr. Moss was the long-suffering owner of the newsagents, which was situated on the Norwich Road at the bottom of Orford Street. He was an amiable man with vast sticking out teeth and with a fag permanently burning in his mouth. What those fumes were doing to me I hate to think. Sometimes, when another boy did not turn up I would do his round as well and would follow a route that took me through Anne Street, Cardigan Street, Alp Street, Oban Street, Anglesea Road, Orford Street and finally Newson Street.

In the early fifties many of the bigger houses in these streets, owned by landlords, became the crowded homes for the many West Indian workers who had come to this country to take on jobs that needed to be done. I was enthralled by these men and admired them for their easy-going grace. To me they were exotic, and I longed to talk to them but they just went on their way to whatever early morning work they had to do. They were separated from us and I could not break the awful barriers that society installed. To me those graceful, quiet and dignified black men were like gods, and I wanted to bow down before them, I wanted to talk to them, perform tricks for them like a pet dog. But no contact was ever made with these handsome men who worked all day and came home to their crowded homes that were empty of family life because at this time no women were coming to Britain from the West Indies. Of course, I heard the racist bleatings from my father and others who were only too ready to reject contributions from immigrants. While I held black men in high esteem my father regarded those same men as being subhuman. Unfortunately, racism continued to damage our relationships with immigrants right up to and beyond the 1960's and on one occasion, after I had been married to Barbara for about two years, we were so sickened by advertisements in local newspapers advertising accommodation for renting which stipulated 'no blacks' that we put our own advertisement in the paper at a time when we had a spare room in our first home. It read: "Sorry no pets or Tories." Our perhaps futile effort at combating the racism that existed in those times.

Another thing at school that seemed to be very damaging to many boys was that after year one the year was virtually streamed into four classes: 2A1, 2A2, 2B1 and 2B2. Boys in the 'A' classes were considered to be potential university material while the others received a less academic curriculum. The effect of this was that by the end of year five nearly all boys in the 'B' classes left school to go on to jobs and apprenticeships in the town while many of the 'A' stream boys went into the sixth form to take 'A' level G.C.E.'s that might eventually lead to university places. In effect our grammar school, and many like them, were failing half of their intake! As a teacher later in life I have always opposed streaming and was lucky enough to eventually teach in a most wonderful secondary modern school that had no such separation.

Later, in my professional life as a lecturer at a Teacher Training College, I conducted a piece of research over a period of three years in which I examined the verbal interaction between boys and girls in small mixed ability groups as they discussed poetry and prose extracts that had been read to them by me. I recorded all the discussions of two of the groups of pupils, one being led by me as the teacher and the second being pupil-led with no teacher present; the poor control group had no opportunity to discuss the literature that had been read to them. The two groups that were given time to discuss were swapped throughout the research so that they had equal time in both the teacher and pupil-led groups. I transcribed all the recordings and then analysed each utterance at 3-second intervals to see what was going on during the talking. The three groups were given a test three days after the discussions. Not surprisingly both the teacher and pupil-led discussion groups scored significantly higher than the group that had no discussions. However, the teacher-led group's test results when measured showed no superiority at statistical levels of significance than the pupil-led. Although I was principally interested in the kinds of verbal interaction that went on in the two groups when they were teacher or pupil-led, it soon became obvious that in both groups the more able pupils (as measured by several pre-research tests for verbal fluency, reading etc.) benefited when having opportunities to explain to their less able counterparts; and the less able learned from their possibly more able peers. This was more so when the groups were pupil-led and could use their peer group forms of interaction more freely. As a result of this research, I was encouraged in my teaching to continue organising my classes into small mixed ability, pupil-led groups.

My research also suggested that those who argue for rigid streaming in schools base their beliefs solely on *teacher-led classes* where pupils for the most part sit in silence thus stifling any pupil-led verbal interaction of the kind that stimulates active learning. In other words, mixed ability classes can only show their superiority when they are organised along pupil-led groupings, where, I believe, the most active kinds of learning occur. It is indeed unfair to compare streamed and unstreamed classes when the method of teaching is traditional teacher-at-the-front, semi-lecturing. When pupils are given a chance to learn through discovery and by asking their own questions rather than answering the teacher who remains sole arbiter, then the bright children can learn effectively by explaining to their less able peers in genuine peer-led talk. Incidentally, in the sixth form at Northgate much learning went on when we sixth formers were discussing among ourselves – in the common room, at break, in the library, and in our free time. For example, I can still remember John Randall, a bright, athletic boy who played wing in the rugby team, holding forth in the library about women being equal to men (this was 1955). Later on, when we were revising for 'A' levels I benefited enormously from conversations with Peter Morcom and Brian Reade as we took our breaks from the magnificent Ipswich Reference Library and sat drinking mugs of tea in a little street cafe. But I am rushing ahead again! I just want to add that I shall return later to a more detailed analysis of the language of the classroom when I refer to my M.Sc. research project.

In the fourth year I befriended a new boy named Tony Green. What was special about Tony was his ability on the sports field. He came to the school in the rugby season and on the afternoon he first played rugby with us we were overwhelmed by the pace at which he played the game. He was truly outstanding in every part of the game, handling, passing, running with the ball, and scoring. He was handsome and blonde with a very powerful body. He scored a whole bag full of tries and I could see our sports master was very impressed. Tony walked straight into the school's colts' team and then in to the school's second team. This was unheard of for a fourth-year boy: he was playing with sixth formers and starring at their level.

He and I became good friends, and I shared his passion for the other game, football. We used to go and watch Ipswich Town players train pre-season and I remember Tony bringing his girlfriend to these occasions. While we three fooled around I can remember being puzzled at some of the secret jokes the other two shared. I was a complete innocent as far as girls were concerned and longed to be in on the secrets the other two shared. They used a phrase 'ringing the bell' which sent them into paroxysms of laughter and it wasn't until years later that I realised that this phrase referred to her orgasms. My lack of knowledge about girls' sexuality made the two of them laugh even louder.

Tony preferred football to rugby and was keenly sought after by some good local teams and matters came to a head when later on, in the fifth-year season, Tony refused to play rugby for the school because he wanted to concentrate on his football skills with one of the local sides. This brought him into conflict with the school staff and headmaster who saw his refusal to play for the school as a lack of loyalty. He was threatened with expulsion but refused to play for the school and was duly expelled. I was shocked and hurt but Tony went out of my life from then on. He was a remarkably confident athlete and he seemed to have everything going for him but deep, deep down there was something seriously sad about Tony which I could not fathom. Later on, I could not help matching him with the hero of Scott Fitzgerald's book "The Great Gatsby". Somehow it seemed to me that Tony was not going to make the really big time he seemed destined to achieve, and indeed I think this is how things turned out in the end: he didn't reach stardom in professional football, and I don't know what became of him. One thing has stayed with me forever concerning Tony Green and that is the knowledge of just how good you have to be to reach the top in any sport. I think of international footballers, cricketers or athletes and I know that you have to be *Tony Green plus* to get there. For example, Alastair Cook who, to me, is one of the best batsmen England has ever had, used to score hundreds for his school team and I know that scoring a century was way beyond anything that any boy at Northgate scored in my time there. My highest was 49 and that was against a Suffolk third team.

I didn't know it at the time, but my life was about to change in certain ways that would put me on a path that would be utterly different from anything that anybody who knew me could have predicted. I was heading for an early fifth year exit from school alongside my other friends in lower stream classes, but instead ended up completing three years in the sixth form and thereafter the pursuit of an adult life that distanced me entirely from those local Ipswich jobs, apprenticeships, and companies that my immediate contemporaries pursued in most cases for the rest of their lives.

What changed me? I think the first inkling was when I was in the second year, and I was asked for the first time to write a piece that had some relevance to my life outside school. I didn't know it at the time, but I had some aptitude for writing personally and I chose to write about Siamese fighting fish that a neighbour of ours kept in his aquarium. I was impressed with these fish as the males were so decorative with their blue and black colouring and long, flowing tails. They were aptly named as they would sometimes fight to the death, especially if there was a female present. Our neighbour, Jim, had to keep the two males he had apart by inserting a rectangular piece of glass in the aquarium and for my entertainment he would occasionally take this partition out and let the males have a go at each other. My piece of writing was about these fish and their fighting capabilities. My form master at the time was a Mr. Fensom who liked the piece so much that he arranged for it to be included in the annual school magazine. That was that for a couple more years. I was surprised but didn't think any more about it.

A much more significant event occurred in one of Mr. Weight's lessons when I was in the fifth year. Mr. Weight taught English to us reluctant learners and like most other teachers had some difficulty in controlling us. However, he was an impressive figure and would entertain us with his stories of the Second World War when he had been in the RAF and stationed on one of the Maldive Islands. He had obviously loved his experience there and was able to convey the great beauty of these islands to us schoolboys. He was a tall, sallow man, very thin, with a hooked nose and the bluest chin I have ever seen. He would have made an excellent Captain Hook! The thing about Mr. Weight was that he loved his subject, English Literature, and this is what eventually impressed me most. One day he came into the classroom waving a small piece of paper triumphantly at us and telling us that he was holding something that was the most precious thing he had ever handled. We boys were taken aback and immediately hooked. What was it? He explained that it was a short letter written by Thomas Hardy and that was why it was priceless. He then went on to describe Hardy and his work and by the end of that lesson I resolved to go to the library and get one of Hardy's novels out to read. The one I chose was 'Jude the Obscure'. I didn't say anything to Mr. Weight but took the book home and read it from cover to cover in about a week. I loved the sadness in the book and the characters and, above all the way Jude and his family fought for their rights only to lose against an oppressive regime dominated by the ruling class, landowners, bosses, academics and the church. When I told

Mr. Weight I had read Jude the Obscure he was taken aback – I think more by the fact that I had obviously got so much from it despite it being, in his opinion the last of Hardy's novels that should be read owing to the darkness of the author's vision in those pages. However, he was pleased by my enthusiasm and suggested I read a lighter novel such as "Under the Greenwood Tree." In fact, I went on to read all Hardy's novels in the space of a few weeks. I was already climbing out of the wood in which I had been lost for four years.

My sporting career continued to flourish at school: in the fifth year I came third in the cross country and a photo of the first three boys appeared in the local Evening Star. Our sports master came to show me the photo and made a remark that I have never forgotten and which, in my later years, made more sense. He jokingly referred to me as being handsome to which we both laughed. On my part because I knew this wasn't true! I learned later that he was quite a strong supporter of the Labour Party. The thing was that he always treated me, I thought, with a certain degree of favouritism. In the sixth form he made me captain of the rugby team, captain of the swimming team, and I obtained colours in all sports. We got on well, I knew he liked me and I always felt special in his company. There are some moments in my life that I look back on with extreme embarrassment and self-hatred. It may be because I had been stupid or nasty or tactless or whatever, but this moment I am about to recall hurts me possibly most of all. I think about it regularly with deep sadness and wish I could eradicate my actions. I had left school, completed national service, and was enjoying a good social life with my contemporaries. I had a job supply teaching and I played trumpet in the popular Ipswich jazz band. It was 1957 and the young people were rejecting the popular music of the day in favour of a jazz revival of New Orleans music. Incidentally, I frequently point out that popular music in the early 1950's was listened to by parents not their adolescent children who hated songs such as "How much is that doggy in the window/the one with the waggely tail". Popular music was played by tired British bands and fairly talentless singers on radio, particularly on Sundays. Programmes such as "Family favourites" and "Housewife's Choice" were never in the same league as 'Top of the Pops', which was to follow in the 1960's.

Anyway, on the night in question I called in to the 'Golden Lion' a pub frequented by leading stars from the Arts school, the jazz lovers and the disenchanted, duffle wearing beatniks. At the bar I saw Mr. Daniels and I know he saw me. I didn't say anything to him as I walked through into another bar, thinking I might say hello later. The thing is I felt embarrassed and felt in my bones that he may have called in specially to see me, word having got around about the jazz fraternity and their meeting place. For some reason I didn't go back into that bar. Was I trying to break free from my school days? I don't know... but I didn't do the right thing for a friend who had been so good to me. Many decades later I mentioned Mr. Daniels to someone who had also attended Northgate School in the late forties, and he responded by shouting out: "The man was a well-known poof!" I remonstrated with the guy and told him to watch

Cross country runners

his language and his prejudices. I was taken aback but I was also reminded of my own bad behaviour to a good friend, a man I now know I sort of loved and should have returned his friendship by greeting him and having a chat over a pint. I must have hurt Mr. Daniels badly as he stood lonely at the bar by himself. When I went back to that bar he'd been standing at he had gone. For ever out of my life.

The Sixth Form

I was saved from the life I was heading towards when, in September 1951, I entered the sixth form in order to take a couple more G.C.E.s. I had passed in only four subjects and needed the other two to give me some semblance of success. Fortunately for me I was in the first intake to sit G.C.E.s rather than the old School Certificate, which I would have failed as candidates had to pass in a broad range of subjects. The new G.C.E. examination opened up education for a greater number of students, including adults, who could pass individual subjects at different periods in their life. I, for example, was able to take and pass 'O' level geology when I was doing National Service, and at the age of 72 I passed 'O' level equivalent in French. My dread is that the present conservative government seems hell bent on introducing a kind of baccalaureate system that will, in essence, take us back to the bad old days when education came to a full stop if you didn't pass a *wide range* of subjects at the first go.

I loved the sixth form from the moment I entered it. Not only was I able to take my other two 'O' levels but I also sat in with the 'A' level boys taking English Literature. Here I met for the first time a new set of friends who actually *enjoyed* learning. Mr. Weight had done his stuff and I was now able to extend my passion for Thomas Hardy's novels to other forms of literature. The great break through occurred principally because the main English teacher was Peter Hewett. Again, I felt he was a teacher who liked me and recognised my somewhat innocent enthusiasm which shone through my ragged and clumsy efforts to come to grips with the academic rigour and ability with which my fellow students approached their work. Peter Hewett was simply a great teacher whose knowledge of literature and indeed all the arts was enormous. He was brilliant in the classroom and his skill in getting students to participate actively in their own learning was extraordinary. We did most of the talking in his classrooms thus actively learning through peer group channels that in the end meant most to us. We were able to do this because Peter was brilliant at questioning and prompting responses from his students. His knowledge was incredible, but he was not simply interested in passing that on to us: he was far more interested in getting us to develop our own intellectual strengths. To this day I can remember individual lessons taught by Peter Hewett, I can see the blackboard on which he had written Hardy's "During Wind and Rain" and how I marvelled as the poem's structure and meaning unravelled through his questioning. I can remember the smell and feel of some of the books that were presented to us: the beautiful white covers of Blake's Songs of Innocence and Experience illustrated by one of Blake's watercolours, for instance. I have an abiding love of all the works and authors we studied with Peter, which included Shakespeare's King Lear, Henry IV Part One, and Midsummer Night's Dream; Jane Austen's Mansfield Park, Blake's Songs, Wordsworth's Prelude, Milton's Paradise Lost, Book 2, Keats' Odes, selected poems by Gerard Manley Hopkins, and many other works beyond the syllabus including T.S. Eliot's "The Wasteland", poems by Wilfred Owen, and other plays by Shakespeare including Henry IV Part Two and Anthony and Cleopatra. We also discussed films with Peter, and he'd take us to see some of the classics at that time. I remember "Marie D'Or" with Simone Signoret and then "Rashomon", which we saw on a visit to London. Peter once gave a talk on the works of Picasso which to my mind was quite brilliant and better than anything I'd heard in the art department.

A number of the works outside the curriculum were taught by Peter in an evening class on Friday evenings he held in the primary school in his home village twelve miles away. A few of us would cycle there throughout freezing winters to join these 'worker's education' classes and then spend a few more hours down the pub and at Peter's home, a converted mill, where he and his wife Diana would talk with us about politics, C.N.D., the arts and – what mattered to us above all – sex and personal relationships. At this point I'd like to quote Trevor Nunn, the theatre director, who was a student two or three years below us at Northgate. Trevor was one of Peter's stars and here, in an introduction to Peter's autobiographical work, "Owslebury Bottom," in which Peter describes his early childhood, Trevor writes:

"Those Friday nights were exhilarating. We were studying, but we were no longer in school uniforms. Not only were the sessions on Shakespeare extraordinarily illuminating because the discussions Peter provoked were inclusively adult, but the atmosphere had a conviviality which at the end of each seminar led us en masse down the dark lanes and into the pub. Peter called us by our first names, we smoked cigarettes, drank beer and talked and talked and talked..."

In the sixth form I always travelled to school by the Corporation tram. I would walk down to the centre of town, Electric House, and catch the bus there. I was lucky because this was always the bus that Peter caught after he had travelled to Ipswich from Kirton in one of the red East Anglian buses. So, he and I would sit together at the top of the tram where he could smoke and, after the ritual offering of a fag to me which I had to refuse being in school uniform, we would chat about all kinds of things. He had this wonderful way of looking at you, full of mirth and mischief, and you couldn't help thinking that he liked and was interested in you above all else at that particular moment. He picked on *your* strengths when he spoke to you and one of my strengths for him was that I was genuinely working class. I found out many, many years later that Peter had been the leading communist student during his time at Oxford. In fact, he nearly persuaded Dennis Healey to join the party at that time. One story revealed to me in those later years was that Peter's student room was invaded by members of the Bullingdon Club who proceeded to destroy his belongings. When he complained to the authorities he was told: "But isn't that what you want to do to them?"

Anyway, Peter used to draw me into his aura of complicit affection by adopting a 'you and me against the others' attitude when he talked about trade unions and working-class aspirations as though my fellow students were not quite in that realm. I remember for instance him looking at me with his lifted eyebrow when some of the more middle-class students asked him what a 'scab' was in relation to a strike that was publicised in one of the newspapers. He had a remarkable ability to combine his essential goodness with wickedly mischievous, anti-establishment opinions and beliefs. Trevor again:

"...how blessed I was, we all were, to have our lives shaped by such a life-loving, life-inducing man...above all the man himself, utterly honest, completely good, unfailingly aware, openly emotional and truly human. Peter loves the moments in literature when what is apparently simple resonates with many levels of meaning. It is, I have always thought, truly appropriate that one of his favourite lines is Hamlet's, summarising his father's life:
    'He was a man. Take him for all in all.'"

Trevor Nunn, 1991

All of this reading, watching, talking, and interacting with my sixth form peers was having an enormous effect on my life and giving me new paths to follow. I was breaking free from rigid thinking about *Ipswich and a 'job for life'* which was prevalent among my friends who left school at the end of the fifth year. I was throwing off past allegiances in favour of what I regarded as a much more interesting life that was not reliant upon radio programmes such as "Family

Favourites" and Geraldo's dance band on BBC or the daily celebrity trash supplied by the gutter press. I began reading the New Statesman, starting to think much more seriously about politics and recognising that ordinary people had it in their power to affect changes in society for the better. I suppose I was at the same time developing into a little creep who thought he knew all the answers. My mother was marvellous throughout: she let me stay on at school when most working-class mums and dads wanted their sons to leave school and start earning. Mum even began to take an interest in some of the books I was reading and she certainly began to go to the Repertory Theatre to see plays. She was always saying to me: "Michael, isn't education a wonderful thing." This coming from a woman whose early poverty was illustrated best by the childhood toys she owned, which consisted of bits of wood that stood in for dolls.

I was also proud of the fact that the other sixth form boys liked coming round to our place where they would meet my sisters. We now lived in a 'posh' council house in Anglesea Road, less than three hundred yards from number 56 Newson Street. We had moved up in the world physically as well as socially. Yes, 19a Anglesea Road became a little mecca for my sixth form mates. They practised very basic jazz and blues and chords on our broken-down piano. My sister Gloria was also an attraction, especially when she danced to the music! She had a most perfect figure and was later employed by the Ipswich Art School as their favourite model. I have learned later in my adult life that some of the male art students in those days had to take frequent breaks because of the effect she was having on them! I always thought it was most odd that some of my mates had seen my sister naked whereas I had never seen her like this in our tiny three bed-roomed home with its Victorian values.

My immediate friends were now those boys who had been 'A 1 and 2' students in previous years, the boys who had worked hard from first to fifth year, who had always completed their homework, always listened to the teacher, and who could see some direction in their lives which would include further education at university or college. I loved talking with them about the literature we studied and about film, the arts, society and, a bit later, New Orleans Jazz. In fact, I was actively learning in peer groups where more knowledgeable and in many cases more intelligent boys were influencing my thinking. Boys like Pete Morcom, Brian Reade, John Randall, and Jimmy Ward were now my friends. At about this time Peter Hewett directed a school production of Midsummer Night's Dream and these boys all had major parts in it. Although I played only a non-speaking part as one of Theseus' guards I entered into the production with zest and appreciation. Where was I going to end up? I didn't know except that I had become so involved that I was going to take 'A' level English at the end of the second year in the sixth form. My sports career was still progressing and included trials at schoolboy county level in both cricket and rugby. Friday nights at the Hewett household continued with analyses of some great poems including Hardy's "During Wind and Rain" and Owen's "Exposure" as well as "Prufrock's Song" and "The Wasteland". I especially loved studying "King Lear" and "Henry IV Part I" and my interest in these plays has continued throughout my life as I have gone out of my way to see productions of them in London and Stratford on Avon over the past 50 years.

I took and passed 'A' Level English, obtaining a Grade 4 and was persuaded by another school friend Peter Lait, to stay on for a third year in the sixth form in order to study for the 'A' level history examination at the end of that year. I shall remain forever in debt to Peter Lait as it was he more than anyone else who persuaded me to stay on at school that third year of sixth form. Peter was a studious, fun loving boy who was also inspired by Peter Hewett. Quite unlike me, Peter was not at all into sport, favouring books and jazz far more. We became very close friends, and I learned a lot from him about ways of reading and listening and talking. He became my best friend and I suppose those teachers who knew us both from our earlier school careers would not have forecast that. I also chose to study 'A' Level Economics at the local School of Commerce. I made the most of the fact that I was studying at the School of Commerce as well as Northgate. When I was not at one of them they thought I was at the other. Sometimes I was at neither and enjoyed a private life that included learning ballroom dancing at The Arlington, a dance school run by the two sisters. These were pretty young women, quite glamorous and highly regarded on the Ipswich scene. I remember clearly how difficult it was for me, a virgin of 19 years, to dance close to the exquisitely perfumed Maureen with body contact, insisted by ballroom teachers, from the waist to the knees, especially in the tango (my favourite dance). I sometimes had to resort to counting in my head or saying the alphabet and then I might lose the rhythm or timing. They did take to me and sometimes I was invited to share their beach hut at Felixstowe when to my dismay they were always accompanied by their grown men friends. I did get a lot out of the dancing and eventually took my silver medal – as did my two older sisters who went on to take gold.

On one occasion I benefited hugely from my attendance at the School of Commerce much to the annoyance and even anger of my friends Peter and Brian. The school old boys association had presented Northgate teachers with a billiard table, which was kept in a special room where some of the staff would play. We took an objection to the fact that a few of the teachers were playing snooker at lunch times. We were of the opinion that they should be working on more learned matters! (I suggested earlier that we could be prigs!) So one evening after school Peter Morcom, Brian Reade and I stole all the billiard balls, wrapped them up in my rugby shirt and hid them under the library floorboards. By lunchtime next day we noticed several staff members going round the school, looking into dark corners and cupboards. We were delighted to view this behaviour proving that our 'jape' was succeeding. (Incidentally, in later life I could always amuse my own children by telling them tales about 'japes' and 'wheezes', purposely using this kind of language as it matched their own understanding of the odd language used by cartoon heroes such as Lord Snooty as portrayed in their comics.) Anyway, the teachers could not find their billiard balls and their frustration was visibly rising during the three days they continued hunting.

Eventually the headteacher said in school assembly that if the missing balls were not returned within a day the police would be called in and the culprits, once identified, would be in for a lot of trouble, I think expulsion was mentioned as a possibility. So it was agreed that Peter and Brian would get up very early next morning, retrieve the balls and return them to the masters' billiards room. I could not join them as I had to go to the School of Commerce for my Economics 'A' level class. The two of them made their way to school and up the path leading to the main doors above which was situated the library. Unfortunately, as they approached the doors they could see the sixth form master looking down upon them from the library window. They had been caught! Subsequently, later that morning they were hauled in front of the head who gave them an extremely severe dressing down. Being at the School of Commerce I missed all this. In the afternoon the two others were extremely bitter that I had got off scot free and insisted that I go to the head and offer my apologies. They forced me to 'face the music.' I went to the headmaster's study, knocked on the door and was called in. I began by saying to the head that I had also been involved in taking and hiding the billiard balls but before I could complete my apology, he shouted: "Oh Wilson, I've had enough of this. Go and find Morcom and Reade and they will tell you what I said." I left the room hurriedly. You can imagine my friends' chagrin when I told them of this! What a wheeze...

This, my final school year, was one of the best years in my life. Jazz was the biggest influence and some of us took up playing instruments. Pete Morcom started on clarinet and then moved to banjo, Peter Lait played trombone, Brian Reade guitar, and I favoured the cornet. Our first efforts were very basic indeed. We tried to play like the early New

Orleans musicians, those who stayed in New Orleans and did not move on to Chicago. Musicians such as George Lewis, Jim Robinson, and Bunk Johnson were listened to time and time again. We wanted to play like them. It wasn't long before we had formed our own band and our first gig was in the village hall at Boxford. We knew three numbers which we played slow, medium, and fast to extend our programme to last much of the evening. A number of students from the Art School joined with us and they helped us decorate a cellar underneath a local Record shop, which became our regular venue. This was the start of the fifties jazz revival as far as Ipswich was concerned. Students had a place of their own to listen to jazz and talk the talk. I worked hard at the cornet and learned many New Orleans numbers, concentrating on the melody line and in fact sticking to that as I found improvisation just about impossible. In reality, I was never good at playing the trumpet – not like some of my friends who had real talent and could improvise at will. Others, and especially Pete Morcom, were more talented and could improvise, harmonise, work round chords and be creative.

Every Sunday afternoon we would gather round Peter Lait's house to listen to jazz and blues classics. We were totally absorbed in it and crazy to learn as much as we could about the great jazz musicians and their music. The George Lewis Band was a favourite and I particularly loved the trumpet playing of Bunk Johnson. Other greats included Big Bill Broonzy, Louis Armstrong, Jelly Roll Morton, Leadbelly, Sister Rosetta Tharpe, Jimmy Yancy, Ma Rainy and many others. What a change from most of our parents who liked popular music such as that played by Carol Gibbons and his Savoy Hotel Orpheans and other 'easy listening' songs that were crooned on BBC! We had our music, our literature, our politics, our artists, and we were going to change the world - and this was only boring old Ipswich!

In fact, the student generation around Britain in the early and mid-fifties was turned on to traditional jazz: not for them the popular music listened to by older generations. When, many years later, as a teacher, I used to tell my students of the sixties that 'pop' music up until the early fifties was all the rage with parents and not their sons and daughters, they would not believe me. This disbelief sprang from the fact that the new sixties younger generation was listening to Bob Dylan, the Beatles, the Rolling Stones and so on while mums and dads continued with their easy listening, now no longer the pop music of the day. A music historian would point out that the music played by sixties rock and rollers was in fact based on the very blues music that my generation listened to in the fifties. Dylan, for instance, has always been steeped in the old blues, jazz, folk and country music of America; and I know that some of the Rolling Stones Band used to listen to Ken Colyer in *Studio Fifty One* when they were young schoolboys in the late fifties and early sixties. Also, John Lennon and Paul McCartney first got together when they formed a skiffle group that would play folk music and blues. Skiffle groups were first formed alongside traditional jazz in the fifties. Most Jazz bands in the fifties had their own skiffle group. Our band was no exception. In the early sixties, for a brief while, skiffle took over more strongly from jazz. For example, once my mates and I had left Northgate School, younger boys in the school started their own skiffle group.

In David Kynaston's brilliant book "Family Britain: 1951 – 57" he writes about possibly the most famous British skiffle singer, Lonnie Donegan whose single 'Rock Island Line' was in the Top Twenty for 19 weeks: "'Rock Island Line' almost overnight started a teenage craze. The keynote was do-it-yourself." All you needed was a tea chest bass, a simple acoustic guitar or banjo, a washboard and thimble and the ability to play three chords in one or two keys. "Over the next three years (56 to 59) skiffle groups mushroomed around the land, including in Liverpool where the Quarrymen, with John Lennon on a cheap little mail order guitar, playing at first mainly in church halls and suchlike." Where I quarrel with Kynaston is that for him skiffle was the music of the early, mid and late fifties when in fact our generation was much more into the jazz played by trumpet, clarinet, trombone, banjo/piano, bass and drums. For us skiffle remained peripheral in comparison with its mother jazz and yet Kynaston devotes no words to Ken Colyer and precious few to Chris Barber and Humphrey Lyttleton while Donegan gets a full page! Kynaston says nothing about the hundreds of jazz bands sprouting up in universities and colleges, towns and even villages. In fact for many of us Donegan was despised for his lowering of standards when it came to the blues and folk music. We were much more into Big Bill Broonzy who played proper blues.

Nevertheless, it can be argued that Donegan's style looked to the future, which would be rock and roll, while we were stuck in the past. Certainly, by the sixties one could argue that the great popularity of traditional style jazz was over for young people who were now listening to music coming from their own generation and homeland and not from New Orleans. That doesn't matter, traditional jazz was like a bridge that enabled us to break free from the crushing boredom of popular music played for mums and dads. Jazz was replaced by a popular music for young people that was new, creative and at the same time at its best, had its roots in jazz, the blues and folk: I mean the rock and roll ballads of the sixties.

Beyond school: 1954 to 1958

Our horizons were extending, and we began to meet up with people who lived as far away as Colchester (18 miles) who shared our interest in jazz. Extraordinary characters some of them were such as Bernard Watson, clarinettist, and artist, who was slightly older and had been a pacifist who refused to do National Service and who had to work in tin mines instead. There was Don Nevard (pianist), a tall, gangly man with a high-pitched voice and pronounced Suffolk accent who owned one of the largest collections of early jazz records in the country. And there was Ida Hughes Stanton, a writer and bohemian who lived in a Tudor cottage in Stratford St. Mary, mid-way between Ipswich and Colchester. Ida was older than us and she drew us into her fold with her hospitality and stories of the thirties. She was supposed to be a distant relative of Robert Graves and indeed wrote a few children's stories under the name of Affleck Graves. Her ex-husband Blair Hughes Stanton had been the man who carried D.H. Lawrence into the sanatorium in southern France where Lawrence died. Wow, what did I think of that! Ida told us that Blair had reported that Lawrence weighed little more than a five-year-old. Other friends of Ida included Lionel Penrose, the art critic, John Pertwee (later to become one of the Doctor Whos), and Barbie Weekly, Freda Lawrence's daughter by her first husband. There were many others and other stories that fascinated us and made us feel we were part of a most distinguished company. We had just been studying some of these people in school and now it seemed we had some kind of secondary contact with that world of famous writers and artists. While our world seemed to be expanding, the possibilities for making our mark seemed to be less distant.

Some came to us, one of them being Tony Dockerill who had been about two years ahead of us at Northgate and left before we entered the sixth form. He had been away from Ipswich and had obviously got interested in jazz himself. He did not know of any others similarly interested until he found Pete Morcom and me when he visited 19a Anglesea Road on hearsay that there were indeed others interested in listening to and even *playing* jazz. I remembered Tony from a speech he gave at a mock General Election held at Northgate to coincide with the 1951 General Election. His speech was quite brilliant, full of analytical thinking and wit. My memory had been exact when it turned out that Tony continued to amuse others with his sense of comedy and sharp intelligence as he became well established in the Ipswich jazz scene. On that first occasion when he turned up at my place Peter and I were playing some newly learned tunes, Pete on banjo and myself on cornet. We could sense Tony's amazement and delight at finding two boys playing jazz in the front room of an Ipswich council house, and when I picked up an old ash tray to use as a mute and blew some wah-wah notes his delight spilled over into laughter. He could not stop, then we could not play for his laughter was catching. Although he could have been laughing *at* us for being so crude in our playing, I don't think it was that: it was rather that he got caught up in our audacity and maybe he could see himself joining us on another instrument at a later date in which case his laughter was from the excitement of the occasion. Indeed, it wasn't long before Tony was playing clarinet as well as making his mark at Ipswich Arts School. What days they were!

Sometime between 1954 and 1956 our band progressed to the title of "The Ipswich Jazz Band and our new weekly venue was at The Gardener's Arms" on Bishop's Hill. This was becoming something else! We were actually beginning to be looked up to as part of the new Ipswich scene! A new band was formed with Peter Lait on trombone, Bernard Watson on clarinet, Patience on piano, Trevor Ling on drums, Reg on double bass, Paul on banjo and me on trumpet. We were rapidly extending our repertoire to the extent that we would be playing two or three new numbers each week. Our audience continued to be mostly students and other young people who had caught the traditional jazz bug from listening to records by a whole new crop of professional bands from all parts of the UK. As I said before, a favourite was Ken Colyer who had achieved fame by jumping ship in New Orleans in order to play trumpet with some of the greats who were still around town at that time. On his return home he formed his own band with Chris Barber on trombone, Monty Sunshine on clarinet, and Lonnie Donegan on banjo. They were an immediate hit with our generation and actually got into the Top Twenty with 'The Isle of Capri' a big and beautifully rounded number played fast. I loved it! At this time Peter Morcom and I went to London to hear the Ken Colyer Band play in some dance hall. It was incredibly exciting for us to hear this music played by Brits. The New Orleans music we loved coming from a group of men on stage playing with such mastery and verve. I can picture the scene to this day.

The Ipswich Jazz Band played regularly at the Gardener's Arms and we had quite a following. At about this time Peter Morcom, Brian Reade and Tony Dockerill joined forces with others to form another band. They preferred a somewhat quieter jazz than that which we were playing, and as they were a talented lot, they soon built up a very musical repertoire. A rival band caused some chagrin and in my particular case I suppose I was hurt because Brian Reade took up trumpet and was soon playing some really nice stuff with a lovely warm tone. There was no doubt that he had a greater musical talent than me. However, the two bands never crossed each other's paths except for one occasion when some of the new band came to the Gardener's Arms one night. As our band had previously been practising a whole batch of new numbers, I made sure that these were played in succession for about an hour - just to rub it in that we were not simply relying upon the standard numbers we all knew. Although nothing was said amongst the band, I sort of felt that Bernard Watson on clarinet was well aware of what I was doing.

Another memorable character in Ipswich at this time was Venice Manley. She was simply beautiful, and it seemed that most of my contemporaries fell in love with her. She was the belle of the ball as far as Ipswich Jazz was concerned. Even more than her beauty, her spirit, her personality, and wild unconventionality captivated all who met her. At the age of 13 a lorry had crashed into her and as a result she lost most of one of her legs. This did not stop her from doing anything she wanted to do, which included being one of the best dancers in Ipswich and a great adventurer who walked the Pyrenees amongst other things – with Brian Reade, who was her boyfriend at the time. I remember one occasion when I arranged to meet Venice at the top of the steps to the National Gallery in Trafalgar Square. In the evening we were going to 100 Oxford Street to hear the Humphrey Lyttleton Band. We were due to meet at 1.30 p.m. and Venice was over three hours late. She knew I would wait. One could not get angry with her once she smiled, linked arms with you, and asked with her eyes what would be our next adventure?

Venice melted everybody's heart and it wasn't surprising to any of us when the trombonist who played trombone with the re-formed Ken Colyer Band, became one of her lovers. There was a time when the Ipswich Jazz Band turned this to our advantage as she became go-between by obtaining chords of jazz numbers from the trombonist and passing them on to us in order that we could extend our repertoire. Venice herself was a very good singer. I think it is worthwhile pausing here to give a brief resume of Venice's extraordinary life, although it goes well beyond the biographical era I am describing. The following description is taken from an obituary I wrote when Venice died at the age of 69 together with some comments from Helen Chadwick, a singer and song writer who worked with Venice in a musical group.

She eventually became a singer in a semi-professional group, a voice teacher, a choir conductor, a composer, and a champion of the gypsies' cause. She used to say that 'music and song were central to her life and she could not remember a time when she did not sing.' Singing for her was...'as natural as breathing and happened almost as spontaneously.' From an early age she remembered performing, tap dancing, putting on pantomime and acrobatic shows. She joined a choir at the age of 11– which became the resident musical group for a radio programme called 'Home at Eight', with Alfred Marks, Hermione Gingold and Richard Attenborough, and she was selected to sing the part of one of the angels in Benjamin Britten's Cantata at the Aldeburgh festival with Peter Pears and Britten himself conducting. In the 1950's she was expelled from school for a petty joke involving the tying on of toilet rolls to all the classroom doors of a quadrangle. She was made to walk down the aisle of the school hall to the stage where she had to hand in her school hat and blazer in front of the assembled pupils then ceremoniously walk through the main school doors and away from the school. It is to the credit of a number of her school mates that, despite the opposing wishes of some of the staff the girls accompanied her to the main gates. I can add here that my sister Gloria who also attended the same school was sent down from the third year to sit in first year classes for a month because she had taken a day off school without permission to go to Covent Garden to see a ballet.

At the time the Ipswich Jazz band was playing at the Gardener's Arms Venice teamed up with Bernard Watson, our clarinettist, and the two of them played and sang the songs of Purcell. Her life took a different direction when she went to Ireland and became interested in the social and educational plight of the tinkers in Dublin. At times she literally fought on the barricades with her then partner, Gratton Puxon. They suffered much persecution including the burning down of a caravan that had acted as a schoolroom for the children. Venice's involvement with the gypsy cause lasted 15 years and included the establishment of the first permanent school in Britain for traveller children, in Redbridge, Essex. This was made possible by a contribution from, among others, the Beatles, and financial and practical support from Yul Brynner, who was always extremely proud of his gypsy origins. Yul Brynner and Venice became good friends.

In 1979 her life took another turn, back to singing and the human voice and she began teaching every summer at the Roy Hart Theatre in SW France. Venice was a lyric soprano and helped to form 'Kite', an accomplished and highly regarded a capella women's vocal group. She fell in love with Georgian polyphony and in 2000 she took over as the conductor and Musical Director of the London Georgian Choir.

Venice rehearsing

Venice was a dazzling personality, full of fun and energy and love, which she shared with scores of people over the years despite encountering many difficulties and challenges in her life, including the loss of her leg in that terrible accident when she was 13 years old, being adopted at a very early age into the wrong environment, and losing contact with her only child, a son who was born to her and her husband Mike Crooks. She and Mike parted in the mid-sixties but remained good friends throughout their life. The light of her spirit rose above everything and everyone who ever met her, or even just watched Venice it was clear that she was a remarkable and vibrant woman. She died penniless but utterly rich in the scores of friends and colleagues who will always remember her.

Much of what I have been describing about the Ipswich scene and the jazz following occurred during my National Service. I was conscripted in October 1954 and served most of my time at Woolwich Barracks. Fortunately, I was able to get home at weekends as I became a clerk in the office that dealt with 48 and 72 hour passes. The sergeant in charge was a very soft man, a weakling whom I could twist around my little finger, so I pressurised him blatantly in order to get weekend passes in abundance. I used to get on the Woolwich ferry on a Friday night, walk to the A.12 and then hitch hike home in my army uniform, which was quickly stowed away once I got into our house!

I am not going to spend much time recounting my National Service experiences as they were so dull. I shut myself off from an institution I had not asked to join and as far as possible I let the army pass me by. I hated the army with all its petty rules, its silly parade ground marches up and down, its bullshit polishing of everything one came into contact with, its mental straight jacketing, its bullying, its general uncouthness, and its main purpose, which was to break young men's spirit in order that they would willingly become fodder for trenches if the time ever came. You can see I hated the army! One of the ways they patted themselves on the back as it were, was by ensuring that every national service man got at least one stripe by the end of their two years. This was supposed to show that each man had achieved some success but was in fact a means of showing falsely that they, the service, had succeeded with each conscript. I am so proud of the fact that I did not receive such an 'honour.'

My life was lived at weekends for the two years I was in the army: I was at last beginning to enjoy the company of women. After all, I had spent my childhood in the company of a wonderful mother, I had grown up with two gorgeous sisters, and a third I'd seen grow from a baby to her early teens. At the age of 11 society had sent me to an all boys school and just as I was overcoming the difficulties that imposed upon my development and was beginning to mix socially with women I was torn from those pleasures in order to spend five days a week in a single sex barracks! I intended making up for this at weekends. I had also been ripped away from a culture which had just given me my independence at the age of nineteen, a culture which included books, music, art, and theatre. I was taken away and placed in a single sex society with no culture apart from learning how to march, to polish, and eventually to kill. Having just studied the horrors of war in literature that included Shakespeare's Henry IV Part I, Wilfred Owen's poems about the 'pity of war' and films such as "All Quiet on the Western Front" I was in no mood to accept the incompetence, the bullying, and the pettiness of loud-mouthed sergeants or the inherited privileges of nineteen year old second lieutenants trained at Sandhurst. As far as I knew, everybody else in the barracks was counting off the days to the end of their military service. I am now frequently surprised when I come across old boys in their seventies who claim they enjoyed National Service. You know the sort who say: "Bring back National Service, it'll make men of them." Yuk! I think I was a man before National Service, I was a former captain of school rugby, an ex-school cross country champion, a footballer who had represented my home town in an international match, an ex-street fighter, a trumpet player in a jazz band. Was I not a man? However foolish? Did I need National Service to prove that? Did I need to fire guns, march up and down, clean my boots every night, salute and accept the bull shitting demands of lesser men in order to call myself a man? Of course not! Yet they kept telling us that our training was for the good of the country and that we were a proud nation who were rarely if ever defeated in war. Readers who might be interested in the National Service might like to look out for a film entitled "The Bofors Gun", which, in my view, captures some of the feel of boredom and bullying that could go on in National Service. In respect, I should add that the National Service I have described here should not be confused with the normal military career services for volunteers that exist today and of which I have no connection. The trouble with National Service was that it consisted of young men who did not want to be there and regulars who didn't want us there anyway.

But let me get off my soap box! In a calmer mood I can tell you of a few incidents in the Royal Artillery basic training camp at Oswestry that epitomise my experiences and will soften the mood somewhat. We were trained in the use of 25 pounder guns which needed the attention of six men if my memory is correct. One of the daily training procedures was to follow a strict line of action should a shell get stuck up the barrel. This involved the hierarchy of six men at the gun and ended with the leader pushing the dummy shell back down the barrel with what I remember as a kind of broom handle. When we finally were taken to the Welsh mountains to fire a real, live round it got stuck up the barrel so all six of us turned as one and ran away despite angry officers throwing their sticks at us. Eventually *they* had to make the gun safe.

We were trained almost daily in fire practice, and I think this was just another arduous, meaningless activity to fill in the time. That it didn't work was proved one night when the officer's mess burned down to the ground while the whole battalion slept through it. There was another occasion when my 'mates' hid my boots (they were placed above the rafters in our billet) and in my desperation not to miss morning parade I wore my crepe sole shoes, fashionable in those days and known as 'brothel creepers'. I looked well enough from the ankles upwards but below it was a shabby mess as my gaiters had no ankle leather on which to perch so they fell in a crumpled state over my brothel creepers. Unfortunately for me the duty sergeant responsible for inspecting the gunners on parade that day was Dixon. He suffered from shell shock due to his real war time experiences and walked with a distinctive nervous jerking of his right arm that poked way back when he was agitated. He actually looked like a rather fat version of Adolph Hitler. When he came in front of me, he looked at my beret first, then my jacket, belt and neatly pressed trousers. All was OK. However, his eyes went down, and he saw my feet! There was a long pause while he chewed his moustache and began to shake. He walked round to the back of me and whispered loudly in my ear that 'You'll be on shit house duties for the rest of your days Wilson!' He then bit me on the ear, not severely but with teeth chattering nervously. I looked to the front, and he came back, pulled my beret over my head so that it looked like a pudding and said (what was always said to new recruits) who had done something wrong on parade, 'You are a moon man, Wilson. What are you?' I replied, as all new recruits were supposed to: 'A moon man sergeant.' He indicated that I was to be booked and then moved on.

But my pièce de résistance was on the mighty occasion the whole battalion plus all the soldiers from the west of England and Wales were involved in a huge operation that would include a mock battle. It was known as *Operation Knock-Out* and we trained for this event for several weeks. Unfortunately for me I had overstayed my initial training at Oswestry because someone had lost my papers. So they didn't know quite what to make of me and made me an Ack-I, which was short for *assistant instructor* (no stripe involved). When it came to the great day, we were to march off into the Welsh mountains we assembled on parade. It was noticed that one of the platoon was missing a strap for his rifle so I was sent to HQ with him to get one. While the two of us waited for the sergeant at HQ stores to get a strap the whole regiment had begun to set off down the road and on returning to the parade ground they had already marched about a quarter of a mile. Thinking on my feet I ordered the new trainee to catch them up and proceeded back to the barrack room and my bed. I spent the next three days reading and listening to the radio. I walked around the almost empty barracks with a limp, and nobody ever questioned me. I obtained my food in the canteen as usual with a few other skeleton staff who were there to maintain the place in the absence of everybody else. I was not missed on Operation Knock-out and to this day I do not know if we won that war!

Supply Teaching

As I indicated above, the *timing* of my personal and social life between the years 1954 to 1958, the order in which events occurred, are uncertain as I write them down here. Although I can remember *what* happened as clearly as though it was yesterday. I do know of course that I was in the sixth form between 1952 and 54 and in the army from 1954 to 56. I was supply teaching for the two years between 56 and 58 and here at last I was engaged in paid work that I found interesting, in fact absorbing.

How did this happen? As I was about to finish my National Service, I was on a train with some friends among whom was Tony Dockerill. The train was heading towards Colchester or maybe London and even before we went through the tunnel that greets each train just as you leave the Ipswich station, we got talking about future jobs. Tony suggested that I might like to try supply teaching. I don't think I'd ever considered teaching before, but Tony explained that schools were crying out for temporary staff and that it was quite acceptable for them to take on unqualified people, particularly if they indicated that they were seriously considering applying for a place at a Teacher Training College. So, it came about that in the week after I completed National Service, it must have been the second week in October, I was interviewed by the Ipswich Education Authority and asked to attend a secondary modern boys' school the next Monday for a further interview with the head teacher. They wanted someone who could teach English and P.E. and given my school experience I thought I sounded ideal for the post. At the interview with the head I was taken on and when I asked when I might start he said, "Come in tomorrow. We need you to teach drama to 2b, the lesson begins at 9.30, immediately after assembly and then you'll report to Mr.

Arnold who will give you the timetable for the rest of the day."

So, I was thrown in at the deep end! I cannot remember how I managed the drama lesson, but I do know that by the end of the week I had become convinced that all I ever wanted to do was teach. I didn't experience too much misbehaviour from the boys – and this was not simply to do with the fact that Mr. Arnold kept a slipper in his desk for beating miscreants: it was to do with the fact that I understood these boys, these teenagers. I knew from where they were coming, and I appreciated their difficulties. I had two models to go by: Mr. Hewett with his love for the subject and his capacity to get the best out of his pupils, and myself, who had been a reluctant learner from the age of 11 to 16. My working class upbringing helped. All I thought I needed were some good books and bright ideas. My ability at sports was also a blessing so I soon fitted in to the PE department, and this was an advantage I think regarding the boys' attitude towards me. I earned some respect – although you could never rest your laurels on it!

Looking back on my supply teaching I think it would be fair to say that I learned some things from my mistakes, and I managed to retain discipline in my classes. However, I do not recommend this 'learning at the deep end' as a good preparation for the profession. Currently on television there is a programme inspired by Jamie Oliver in which a number of celebrities are put in charge of classes of adolescents in the belief that their charisma, ability, or stardom in their *own* profession, whether it be as politicians, actors, television personalities or whatever, will somehow rub off on the kids so that the latter will be inspired to learn. This is stupid and, as it turns out, unsatisfactory. Nothing can replace proper training for any profession, whether it is in law, medicine, teaching, acting or whatever. When I did eventually go to college I learned much, not only about my subjects, English, and P.E., but also about psychology, sociology and general creativity, I learned about the actual craft of teacher-pupil interaction: how to ask the right sort of questions, how to react to pupils' responses, how to manage large groups of children, how to reward pupils' efforts and so on. These don't come naturally just through experience. Teaching is no different from any other profession in that it has a theoretical base which needs to be understood before embarking upon practice. Can you imagine amateurs being let loose in the law courts or hospitals? The same should apply to schools.

I'll give you one example where my ignorance did a lot of damage. There was a boy in one of my classes who could not tell the difference between a *b* and a *d*. He had awful problems reading and writing. Mr. Arnold asked me one day to work with this boy at the blackboard on how to distinguish between *b* and a *d*. I spent the whole lesson writing these letters on the blackboard and practising with the young lad to no effect. The lad was talented enough but could not read or write. The monstrous thing was that I was doing this thing to this boy in front of all his school mates – who were not attending to Mr. Arnold but were surreptitiously watching the boy fail constantly. Of course, the boy was dyslexic and had I been to college I would have known this and I would not have damaged the boy's pride in front of his mates by doing what I was doing out of ignorance. Simply learning on the job means you learn *bad* habits as well as possibly some good! I shall never forget my own frustration at failing to teach the boy and later on – and for the rest of my life – I have looked back on this misguided and cruel experience with shame.

I was enjoying life at work and in the evenings and weekends. Peter Lait was also working at the same school, so we were drawn closer together. Both of us intended going to Teacher Training College. In the meantime, our leisure hours were spent listening to and playing jazz. Many of our weekends were spent at Ida's Tudor house in Stratford St. Mary where again we listened to Don's fabulous record collection and talked and talked about everything from art, literature, politics, CND and so on. The river Stour ran past the bottom of Ida's garden and we used to row down to

Dedham through Constable country in a beautiful Thames punt that she owned. These were great times, shared by many including Venice and her new boyfriend, Mike Crooks, who had been working as a steward in the Merchant Navy. At first us arty lot tended to underestimate Mike because he did not share our educational background or interest in the arts. However, it was not long before I realised that Mike was indeed very sharp cognitively despite his somewhat low tastes! In fact, Mike Crooks became an extremely successful business man later in life and showed a particular talent for house building, which included him dismantling a Tudor house in Ipswich, moving it lock, stock and barrel to a village setting and re-building it there. He managed all the bricklaying, carpentry, electrics and plumbing himself! Everybody thought that Mike and Venice were a mismatched pair, but I could see that Venice was mesmerised by Mike's natural inclination *not* to be impressed by the arty crowd's values. She could not impress him with her unconventional views or her vivacious lifestyle (and he would never have waited longer than five minutes for her at the National Gallery!) He was a handsome blonde guy with a somewhat dark attitude to life. Venice was not going to conquer him, consequently she was captivated.

Politically, I was a communist sympathiser although I never joined the party. I was impressed with Russia's sacrifices in the second world war, I believed Stalin was a great leader, that everything in the Soviet Union was OK and that Russian society was heading for ultimate fairness, the death of the state, an end to money and crime, and a joyful sharing of the land's riches. In other words, I was duped as indeed were a high proportion of left wing

CND March

intellectuals in Britain and other western parts of Europe. I loved Russian novels and films and I immediately appreciated Russian ballet as shown in a particularly popular film of the Bolshoi company performing Giselle that was shown in the UK in the late fifties with Galina Ulanova as principal ballerina. I was also very impressed with the Maxim Gorky Trilogy, which I saw at the Hampstead Everyman Cinema earlier during National Service. I used to meet Peter Lait, who was also posted to a London barracks during national service, and we'd go to the Everyman once a week. A good thing about National Service for me: being posted eventually to Woolwich barracks I was able to go to cinemas and theatres quite frequently. Also, I would go to Ken Colyer's club in Great Newport Street every Thursday. I also studied and passed 'O' Level GCE geology. All of this 'alternative' culture encouraged me to forget the army with all its petty restrictions. I came to life once I'd passed through the guarded gates and fell into a trance when I returned and put on a uniform.

My two younger sisters were still at school and so was my brother Clive who had been born in 1952. We were all still close although our contact with the church was just about over. Gail and Gloria got caught up with the jazz scene and as I said before Gloria became an established model at the local art school. Gail had her mind set on teacher training while Gloria was hoping to make a career for herself in the police force. This ambition was spoiled completely by a chief superintendent who made it impossible for her to continue in the police force because of his sexist attitude which included his strongly held view that women should never be allowed to wear a police uniform or carry out police duties! Gloria had already met her future husband and, as I said before, he was neither a boxer nor a native American much to my disappointment. He, David, was a reporter on the Ipswich Evening Star who was later to lead an illustrious career in journalism, which included editorship of the London Evening Standard, and continued with a regular featured article each week in the East Anglian Daily Times. David was also interested in jazz and took up the banjo and would sometimes sit in with us.

It was 1957, I was 22 years old, still a virgin, desperately interested in girls and, apart from the burden of virginity, life was good; enjoying teaching very much, playing in the Ipswich band was exciting, and I had several mates equally interested in jazz, trying out musical instruments, learning chords and attempting to play (however badly) various jazz classics. This period was nourished by hours and hours of group listening to jazz records. The New Orleans jazz revival was at its height. I didn't know yet that I was about to go through a period in my life which was going to bring me joy for two years but which was going to be followed by despair that was going to last a further two years.

Mick playing jazz

Drawing of Mick by Bernard Watson

Being in love

One night at the Gardener's Arms I fell in love. I saw this girl wearing a tight-fitting oatmeal coloured dress with large buttons in the same material extending down her back and turned to Peter Lait, the trombonist, and said, "How would you like to undo all those buttons?" A typically dumb remark from a totally inexperienced young man of the 1950's whose sexual encounters had been limited and limiting! This girl was dancing and chatting and seemed very bouncy and lively to me. Her excitement was captivating. I was enchanted. I went up to her at the interval and talked to her about this her first time here at the Gardener's Arms, what music she liked and so on. Her name was Louise. I asked her if she'd like to meet me later in the week and she, perhaps feeling amused at being picked out in front of her friends by the trumpeter in the band, said OK.

The next two years or so were the making of me and by the end, my undoing. That might do for a definition of a tragedy. In the early days she and I just explored everything around us and everything about ourselves. The great thing about Louise was her sense of fun and delight in company, and above all her sensuality. I couldn't have found a better partner and as time progressed, I fell deeper and deeper in love. It was my first real relationship, and it couldn't have been better. We were equals intellectually, I think.

In the summer of 1957 Louise's family, she and her mum and dad, Anna and Isaac, were planning to go to Cassis sur Mer for their annual holiday and I was going with them. They had been holidaying in Cassis, which is the first port out of Marseille on the way east towards Nice, for a few years now and had booked a small apartment at the bottom of a hill leading down to the sea. I was going to camp in a field of scrappy pines, which was part of the village cemetery, near an abandoned quarry, maybe about five minutes' walk from the apartment. The quarry was of orange coloured limestone rock for which Cassis had previously been famous because of its strength and durability, witnessed by the fact that the base of the Statue of Liberty was made from it as were the docks of Alexandria much earlier. Also, Cassis was making a famous wine long before the Greeks discovered the little harbour. In 1957 Cassis was the same as it had always been, similar to a Cornish port in those days, a few shops, a bakery, one or two bistros, and many small fishing boats moored in a very small dock and along part of the beach, which was never crowded, and – best of all – there were shoals of fish swimming just a few metres from the sandy shoreline in crystal clear water.

You wouldn't recognise it as it has become like much of the rest of the riviera we know today: blocks of flats, gambling casinos, loads of restaurants and pubs, swimming pools, clothes shops etc. And no fish in the less than clear sea immediately off the coast! Fewer and fewer fish exist nowadays, and the small number of fishing boats moored in the port have to travel a long way out to sea to find them. Cassis is now called a 'tourist town'. In 1957 it was a small fishing port beautifully situated along a coast running towards Marseille consisting of remote callanques: narrow, steep walled inlets accessible only by sea. A quite steep cliff edge loomed down on the port upon which there were the remains of a castle; and beyond which was an even larger cliff known as Cap Canaille, apparently the highest cliff of any country leading down to the Mediterranean, North, South, East or West.

Isaac, Anna and Louise were going to make their way to Cassis by train and bus and I was going to hitch hike from Paris. I got a lift from a lorry driver, a small, compact man who really was wearing a blue and white striped T shirt. He was heading to the South coast beyond Marseille, so I was in for a very long ride. We couldn't speak much but that didn't matter, we liked each other, smiled a lot and I gave him a silver half-crown to remember me by. Eventually he could drive no longer, and we stopped by the roadside just outside Arles, which I knew of because of the Van Gogh story. I pitched my tiny tent in a ditch, and he fell asleep in his cabin. In the morning I woke very early, maybe about 5.00 a.m., and the first sensation was of a glorious heat and the brightest of light from the early sunshine. I looked out and could not believe how beautiful it was, the extraordinary blue sky, and the green, tall vegetation. I hadn't experienced anything like it before: my first trip down south, near the Mediterranean and I knew how Van Gogh had felt when he first arrived there! The lorry was gone. The driver was right to go. Maybe he had looked into my tent and seen I was fast asleep? I think we'll always remember each other.

I don't remember getting to Cassis that day, but it wouldn't have taken long. The campsite was 'unofficial' even though it was within a kilometre of the town centre. Our fires were open holes in the ground. This was, after all, 1957. There were only a very few tents and I set mine up in about seven feet of level ground on what was a pine covered slope leading down to the disused quarry. I remember the smell of the pine trees most, in the afternoon siestas when Louise and I were crammed together in a tent that was small even for one individual, as we embraced for sweet two-hour intervals; the blissful sunshine beating down on the pines that shaded us, we could hear the sound of the sea and the gulls, and it seemed as though we were the only two people in the world.

We would eat dinner in town with Isaac and Anna or at their apartment, talk and drink red wine that was bought from barrels in town. I don't remember ever seeing an actual bottle of wine in those days. In the mornings we met for breakfast and then made our way to the famous Cassis boules area in the middle of town, played boules in the company of vociferous locals, swam, snorkelled, and sunbathed for a few hours. We were both good swimmers and thought nothing of staying in the sea for hour long intervals. Then we'd lunch at a beachside bistro before

Louise and I would retire to the tent for siesta: the sounds of birds, the sea and the breeze drowned by Louise's passion in my ear.

Back in England in September 1957 things began to differ. I was still supply teaching, but this couldn't go on forever: there was a two year limit to how much you could do. I had not earned a place in higher education and Louise was going to start Teacher Training that September. Isaac and Anna were always kind to me, but I was aware that they could not see any future for the relationship between Louise and myself. To tell the truth, neither could I much beyond waiting to apply for college myself and getting better at jazz. Louise's family were typically interested in achievements, and I wasn't achieving anything. I don't think any of this was ever spoken about but some of it showed itself in Louise's growing interest in her painting. She wanted to be an art teacher like her father I suppose. Well, she was looking forward very much to college, and this would or could mean a new life. We still did much together, passion was still pursued hungrily and achieved in our normal way, and I suppose I thought this was enough? Before the new academic year had hardly got going, I did get a place, seemingly a life time away, at college – but this wasn't for next September when Louise would be going but for the year after, 1959. I would therefore be lagging behind her by two years.

Bad times were to follow. Louise went to teacher training college, and I continued in Ipswich, supply teaching and playing jazz. I taught at the all-boys secondary modern school and soon realised that I was good at the job. I spent bags of energy preparing my lessons, which I always aimed to be interesting, and I sensed that the headmaster approved of my work. However, there were bad lessons learned at the all-boys school that included too much emphasis on discipline and not enough in my opinion on the treasured pleasures of learning. Another big change was coming however as my period of supply teaching was coming to an end and I had nothing in line for future work, except nine months of waiting until I was going to college. Louise was working her socks off at college and my prospects were very dim. She was drifting away from me, and I was desperately aware that she and her studies could lead to a break-up. What could I do? In desperation I turned to the idea of voluntary work abroad and Louise and her parents thought this was a good idea, making a clean break during which everybody could get on with their own lives and that we would be able to re-assess our future the next September when I would start college. In reality however, I think I was aware that such an arrangement would end in a separation Louise and her family would welcome and I would hate.

Voluntary work

The voluntary work was great. I participated in earthquake repair damage to the roofs of houses in St. Paul in the south of France, hard work but getting myself in trim and a tan! Then I went on to flood repair damage in northern Italy which involved filling wire nets with stones to prevent a river from overflowing. I loved this outdoor existence and got on well with many students from different countries from round the world. I befriended a beautiful young woman from Algeria named Thérèse. Eventually she and her girl friend and I hitch hiked down to Naples to stay with some of her family. Our relationship was entirely platonic, and she would be heading back to Algeria to meet up with Georges whom she was marrying in the autumn. I enjoyed the stay in a working-class area in Naples, in a flat on the third floor where all goods and food were delivered in baskets that were hauled up to the balcony and payments were lowered to the street. I remember particularly being driven by Thérèse's uncle and aunt through Naples at a crazy pace and, they, sitting in the front with him driving. At one stage they both stood up and embraced as they passed the church where they had been married! The car just carried on – thankfully in a reasonably straight line!

It was time for Thérèse to make her way home to Algeria and this meant we had to hitch hike from Naples to the northwest of Italy, and then on to Marseilles for her to catch a boat. This was now August and I knew that Louise, Isaac and Anna would be in Cassis next door to Marseilles, so I arranged for all of us to meet up there, not appreciating that the coldness Louise's family was feeling towards me had grown in intensity, Louise had moved on and was waiting to return to her second year at college, and for them my relationship with Louise was hanging on a thread. Turning up with a beautiful woman did not help matters and Thérèse could feel the bad feelings that were churning around. I remained innocent of how it might have looked with me turning up with a beautiful woman, but I was totally blameless as I could think of nothing else but my love for Louise and the panic in my stomach as a result of the coldness that existed in the atmosphere. We saw Thérèse off on her ferry and I had just one night camping in my usual spot and then a full day's bus tour around the area next day with Isaac, Anna, and Louise. My God! Things went disastrously wrong as I overslept in the tent and missed the tour bus I was to catch with the family! This was to be the end! I did catch up with them at the end of the day, but they were not speaking to me. I was shattered physically and mentally. The family was cold and silent, and we said terrible goodbyes the next morning. I knew it was the end. They were going home and I, too, was to head back to Ipswich with nothing in mind except my despair at losing Louise.

There were one or two messy encounters during the final two months before Louise was due to go to college, but she was adamant that the show was over and she had her college work to think about. I did have one memorable encounter with her mum, Anna, who was lovely towards me and deep, deep down I felt she still approved of me. But it was no use: when a love affair is over it's over. I had to look to the future. I stayed with Mike and Venice in Colchester and found labouring work with Mike. This was the best thing for me as I began the slow process of recovery. Later in the spring of the new year I went abroad again to work for the Service Civile International, this time in Switzerland and then in Greece. I got extremely fit and physically hard. In Switzerland we were building a milk pipeline which involved a climb up a 3,000 foot mountain each day, digging a trench downhill and then a fast run back to the base each night. I loved the camaraderie of the work camp, and it was a great experience to have before starting Teacher Training College in October 1959.

Barbara

I was ready for college, and I think my experiences as a national serviceman, supply teacher, building site labourer and voluntary service worker in previous years gave me advantages over the eighteen year olds straight from school. I found the academic work a pleasure and for the first time in my life began to succeed in written work. I was even awarded top marks at times and took particularly to the courses in Shakespeare, nineteenth century novels, modern poetry, and 20th century drama. I also excelled in the college sports teams, particularly football and cricket. I was in a seventh heaven topped eventually when I met the young woman who was to become my life partner for the next sixty years and more.

How lucky I was to meet Barbara at college! She was an eighteen-year-old straight from school, endowed with incredible talent that initially I did not appreciate, which has continued to flourish over the decades bearing fruit even now when she is almost eighty year's old! It is no exaggeration to say that through her work she has become a person renowned at *world* level. To save time I am going to quote from a preface to one of her most recent books (printed with permission from Routledge). It will give the reader an idea of the magnitude and success Barbara has achieved in her professional work during our marriage and her busy motherhood.

"If you came across Barbara Wilson in 1970 you would have met a 30-year-old married woman, a hippy, Bob Dylan fan, and mother of three children aged five, six and seven, married to a school teacher, living in rented accommodation, owning no house, no car, not even a fridge! Her family was struggling. Things were about to change in 1971 however, as she was about to start

'A' Level Psychology, the first year in which this subject had been offered at this level in England.

Meeting her nearly fifty years later she is a clinical neuropsychologist who has worked in brain injury rehabilitation. She has published 27 books, 201 peer reviewed papers, 123 chapters and 8 neuropsychological tests. She has won many awards for her work including an OBE from the Queen in 1998, for services to rehabilitation; five lifetime achievement awards, one from the British Psychological Society, one from the International Neuropsychological Society, one from the National Academy of Neuropsychology, one from the Encephalitis Society and one from the NHS 70-year anniversary parliamentary awards where she was regional champion for the Midlands and East Region. In 2011 she received the Ramon Y Cahal award from the International Neuropsychiatric Association. In 2014 she received an honorary degree from The University of Cordoba, Argentina. Also, in 2014 she received the M.B. Shapiro award from The Division of Clinical Psychology (affiliated to The British Psychological Society) for Distinguished Contributions to Clinical Psychology. In 2019 she received the annual award from the Spanish Clinical Neuropsychological Society. She is editor of the journal "Neuropsychological Rehabilitation" which she founded in 1991 and in 1996 she established the Oliver Zangwill Centre for Neuropsychological Rehabilitation. A rehabilitation centre in Quito, Ecuador is named after her. She was at one time president of the UK Encephalitis Society and was on the management committee of The World Federation of Neuro Rehabilitation. The UK Division of Neuropsychology has named a prize after her, the 'Barbara A Wilson prize for distinguished contributions to neuropsychology'. She is a Fellow of The British Psychological Society, The Academy of Medical Sciences and The Academy of Social Sciences. She is honorary professor at the University of Hong Kong, the University of Sydney and the University of East Anglia.

She has held 30 research grants. Her work has resulted in changes in clinical practice. For example, as a result of a randomised control trial evaluating a paging system to improve the everyday functioning of people with memory and planning problems, the local health authority set this up as a health care system for people throughout the United Kingdom."

("The Story of a Clinical Neuropsychologist", Barbara A. Wilson, Routledge 2020).

In the first ten or so years of marriage my career as a teacher dominated and Barbara's life centred on motherhood. I found my calling when I began teaching at Monkwick County Secondary School in Colchester, Essex. I was made for this, my personal and educational experience directed me towards it. I think my own wretched schooling for the first five years of grammar school followed by exposure to wonderful teaching at sixth form level prepared me for a teaching style that got the best out of initially reluctant learners. I loved the kids and wanted the best for them. The headteacher at Monkwick, Aubrey Green, was a perfect leader for me: he was a Quaker who practised democracy with both the pupils and staff. What I liked best in him was that he would allow his teachers to go their own way in their individual classrooms as long as it worked, results were productive, and the pupils were reasonably happy and co-operative. In other words, he did not impose a methodology on us teachers or a rigid discipline on the kids. For example, anyone entering my classroom would find the pupils sitting in small groups round tables participating

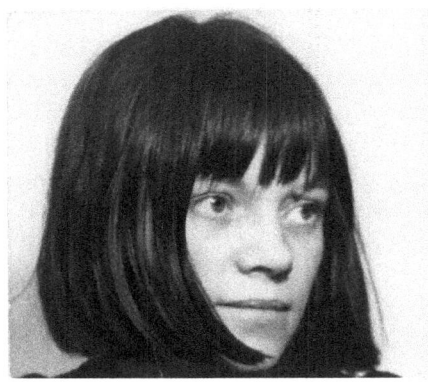
Barbara

in small problem-solving groups much of the time whereas in Mrs. So and So's classroom next door, the pupils might be sitting in rows listening to the teacher much of the time. Most of all, the school was a happy one and the staff in general were committed to the pupils and to their subject disciplines. The school was full of hope and did not suffer too badly from its label of 'secondary modern' which, in society's estimation at that time, meant it was an institution designed for failures. I hope in the next few pages I will be able to render that estimation null and void as far as Monkwick was concerned. We were helped by a lenient national system that existed in the early 1960s which allowed teachers in secondary modern schools much freedom to develop their own curriculum. The new Certificate of Secondary Education, the C.S.E., allowed teachers who were brave and committed enough to take charge of examinations for sixteen-year-olds in their own schools. This meant that for many schools with a dedicated staff the curriculum could be matched to the neighbourhood, making it particularly relevant to the lives of the pupils and their families. I must point out however that this situation did not occur in the majority of secondary modern schools which remained set in their old ways of non- creativity, rigid discipline for its own sake, and bored and unruly pupils who did not find any fulfilment through academic work or creativity.

There were however some star secondary modern schools in the UK that went largely unrecognised for their worth. Ironically, their staff rooms were frequented by many ex-grammar school pupils who went to universities and some of the excellent teacher training colleges that were being extended and which taught child psychology and the sociology of education as well as subject disciplines which seemed to be the main work going on in universities. Also, the teaching profession benefited from the publications of some highly talented university lecturers who published books and papers on teaching methodology. For instance, I can think of James Britton, Douglas Barnes, David Holbrook and the Rosens whose work on pupil participation in the language of learning was immensely helpful to teachers of English.

If we were lucky, and I was, teachers could benefit from the system of teacher inspection which was based at local authority level. It was a system in which teachers and inspectors worked together to improve teaching content and methodology; and actual inspections were not the be all and end all of their existence as seems to be the case nowadays. English teachers at secondary level in Essex in the sixties were particularly lucky in having David Carruth as leading inspector for the discipline of English. I recall one example of his influence when he bought several copies of Douglas Barnes' "Language, the learner and the school" - 1974; sent a copy to each head of English in all the secondary schools in Essex with a directive to read it and be prepared for a meeting in Chelmsford when the implications for teaching English in Essex schools would be considered. I can remember how the sparks flew at that meeting and how fulfilling it was to meet up with teachers from other schools, all of us wanting better results for learning in our classrooms.

I would like now to take the reader into my 1960s and 70s classroom at Monkwick in order to meet some of the pupils and share in their work. I think the best way will be to create a particular week's timetable and the resultant writings will be the actual ones selected from an anthology I collected at Monkwick in that decade. The speech will be selected from a research project I completed when analysing the language of learning in small groups of pupils which I recorded and transcribed for a master's research degree I completed in the 1970s. So, the writings are *from the classroom* and the discussions are *from research that is related to the classroom*.

Language and Learning in the Classroom

Monday morning and I've been working on a theme with my fourth-year class on Desert Islands. Central to the theme is 'Lord of the Flies', one of their C.S.E. books they've been reading as a class reader for several weeks. Over the weeks we've also been referring to Defoe's, "Robinson Crusoe"; collecting pictures of islands beaches, lagoons etc.; and reading poems about the sea and islands. This morning I'm going to play to the class Debussy's "L'apres midi d'un faune" and I'm going to ask them, whilst listening, to write imaginatively about a day in their life alone on an island from dawn to dusk. The idea is to collect in all individual pieces and select something from each pupil in the class to make one long script about a day on an island; record this one extended piece, add island sound effects (gulls, waves etc.), play Debussy's music in the background and make a simple broadcast entitled "A day on my Island". Pupils will be asked to use their five senses when writing and listening to the music. Here is the class piece, which we made into an audio cassette that we sold to their parents. I would hope that some of you readers might be able to play the actual Debussy piece when doing so.

The Island
Look, stranger, on this island now
The leaping light for your delight discovers...
(W.H. Auden)

"The dawn is breaking. This strange feeling of being on an island alone lingers in my mind. I cannot sleep. The air is full of the beachy smell of dried-up driftwood, and of the shrivelled, slinky, green seaweeds which are washed ashore. The sun's forks of light grasp the horizon as it pulls itself from the sea. To the right the impetuous salt water

comes rushing in to the rocky lagoon where the corals in the clear water beam their brilliant colours, and small, darting fish swim in shoals making the sea appear green and red.

The slender palms are still. In the distance, glistening and grand, the surf surges vigorously on to the cold and sparkling shingle with the ever-decreasing pound which echoes down the sands as far as the ear can hear. As I walk up the beach, the footprints behind me remind me of my past life and the clear sand in front, with the high ridges, the life in front of me. Everything seems so sleepy: the birds squawk and flutter as they fly lazily above the lifeless trees, The island, surrounded by water, is cleansed from all sides. The pink rocks which ascend from the shore seem to be a great mass of quivering jelly in the heat haze.

As I enter the interior, rays of yellow and gold fluorescent sunlight flash through the green undergrowth. The ground is a carpet of blue and violet flowers sparkling like big, blue sapphires in the early dew. Palm trees stretch to the blue sky. Like paper blown in the wind, big butterflies unhindered by people. The roots of trees tangle like frozen serpents through the green and yellow undergrowth which also reaches for the blue yonder. Through the mass of jungle thickness silence is spread all around. From on high a stream meanders down, twisting through the rock, then leaping angrily into a swirling, foam filled pool. The shimmering sunshine settles on the cool flux of the stream which flows like the swiftness of a bird. I touch it, so cool, the spray hitting my body and soothes my blistered skin. Crushing down the hardened leaves, creatures move forward and lie beneath the fridgery coolness of the tall green palms which stand surrounded by mountainous cliffs.

As the phosphorous sun reaches its highest point in the sky the jungle, with its bracken hanging out, turns to a splendid array of greenery. The vines seem to be waving as their slender, rubbery arms wrap around trees, strangling the sap from the horny bark. The tendril foliage hangs over the trees like a giant net spread out for miles. Only a few of the rays of sunshine, bright as furnaces, enter the net of foliage to lighten the gloomy atmosphere. Now and again, I notice gay colours of still birds and the flashes from exotic flowers.

Another day begins to pass and as I emerge from the forest, I notice a bird taking wing and gliding gracefully across the evening sun. The waves lap at the shore as they try to get nearer at each turn. Seaweed and driftwood float in on the evening tide. The seaweed spreads its tentacles and reaches for the wood, but the motion of the waves takes it even further – like someone trying to reach for memories but finding none.

Dusk comes. All is quiet. The grass sways in the night wind. The trees move and seem to whisper as they come closer together. All I can hear is the sea washing on the shore, making the stones rub together as they rush backwards and forwards with the tide."

(4th Year C.S.E.)

As far as I know this kind of project where the pupils are not competing but working towards a group achievement involving writing, speech production, editing, and recording is rare. I am most impressed when I recognise influences from other work pupils have done during the year. For example, there are some phrases here that could only have come from a reading of 'Lord of the Flies' (the pink, quivering rocks), the reading of the poem 'Dover Beach' – (stones rushing backwards and forwards) – and even Macbeth (making the sea appear green and red). And, of course, there is the inspiration coming from a superb piece of music. Another cassette I remember was completed during a project on War and Peace when each individual in the class had to imagine they were a German soldier trapped in the snow and ice of Stalingrad writing their last letter home as they faced inevitable death. The final letter was recorded to background noises of modern battle and a suitable piece of music. Again, the tapes were sold to mums and dads as well as contributing to course work assessment.

I think this kind of cooperative work amongst students who are supposed to be competing with each other at their age is rare in Britain and is good preparation for the world of work when they will need to be able to cooperate with professional colleagues.

Learning from the good work that had been practised in primary schools, we encouraged the public display of pupils' writings on classroom walls and corridors, libraries etc. In the very early sixties this was not common in secondary schools although now of course it is prevalent. This is how our system worked. Students were encouraged to re-draft their original work, – looking to correct grammar and expression in special re-drafting lessons. At this stage the teacher would be going round the classroom answering queries and helping out with the technical side of writing. In this way students were learning *realistically* about grammar rather than the boring rote learning that went on in traditional classrooms when grammar was taught *separately from* actual writing and was frequently soon forgotten. I used to say to the students that one of the best aids to writing powerfully, beautifully, and grammatically was the waste basket! One learns to swim by swimming, and one learns to write while writing. The students were also encouraged to illustrate their work and eventually all their work was kept in personal folders on which teachers based their evaluation of course work. Nowadays of course we have computers thus doing away with waste bins in favour of instant changes on screen. To finish this section on writing I'd like to remind readers that in most schools preparing for exams, even today, written work by students is completed in a one-off manner, the work is handed in to teachers, who then mark it (usually in red) and it gets handed back. The student gets a reader of only one, there's no public display or joy in writing, just judgement!

One caveat in my classes was that once a piece of writing was ready for display there should be no mistakes or grammatical errors. I used to get so angry with so-called 'innovative' and 'progressive' teachers who, in their rush to cover their walls with expressive work by pupils, didn't care about *accuracy* of expression or *correctness*. A displayed piece of a child's writing on a wall, with bad spellings and inaccurate grammar used to drive me mad and I felt an urge to tear it down. We should not give more traditional teachers one chance to knock us off our pedestals! Here's a couple of poems I displayed in my fourth-year classroom.

An anonymous poem by R.C. (Thirteen?)

I sit for endless hours
Of well told stories.
My dad, my dad, my dad.
First, it's Russia then Australia.
Now he's under mortar fire.
I sit there taking words and
  sentences in,
Wondering when I may retire.
But it's on and on it never stops.
I wish, if only I could turn him off.
But it's easier said than done.
Television's good but that's no use,
The film's on, "Lost in the desert"
But my dad, well he's in Iceland –
By gad, I've had it!

(Anon, 13 years)

Machinery

Cold black hideous,
Cold black hideous steel
Clanking throbbing bobs and gadgets
Rending bolts pumping pushing -
Cold black and hideous.

Feed its mouth brassy and hot
Feed its mouth with intelligence
Give it more knowledge, train its brain
Feed its mouth, with life.

See if it can walk,
See if it can walk the floor unaided
Beckon it, call it
See if it can walk to you.

Take it outside
Take it outside and show it the world,
Show it mankind death and hatred
Take it to the world outside.

Teach it death and hatred
Teach it death and watch its gadgets throb,
Why does it cower at us? It's more intelligent?
Quick teach it death and hatred.

Even he cannot learn
Even he cannot learn the art of death
We only know this art alone
Even he cannot learn.

Leave the thing at peace
Leave the thing we have tried to teach.
It had the power to overthrow us all;
Don't teach it all we know.
Cold back and hideous - leave the thing at peace.

Kay Quigley 3III

(This poem was mentioned on the BBC programme "Books, Plays, Poems" when its considerable power and skill were commented on.)

A piece of prose

I walked home along the cold, dark road. It was a cold night with the stars shining occasionally through the clouds. I was cold and hungry. I began to think about what I might have for tea: soup, steaming hot, with sausages and potatoes covered in thick, brown gravy. A nice cup of tea, and to finish up with some hot, sweet rice. These thoughts made me hungrier and made me hurry. The thoughts went round and round. My mouth was full of these tastes and it watered so much that I had to swallow it. I could see my house now, so faster and faster I went. I reached the back door. I opened it and there on the gable was a plate of sandwiches with a note saying, 'I have gone to Miss Smith's funeral,' Mum."

Colin Tucker, 4.I

(All three pieces were first published in the school magazine in1966)

I have written extensively about the language of learning in my classroom, arguing for greater pupil participation, and providing examples of pupils' creative writing and speech. However, there is one area where I am of the opinion that we did not do so well in the 1960s and have continued to fail in modern times when it comes to encouraging debating skills and more impersonal writing that requires competence when arguing one's own case or point of view. Without such skills we are at a disadvantage when it comes to exercising control over our own destinies. Here I think is where teachers can play a more dominant role in teaching expertise in the actual grammar of debate, whether it be written or spoken. I'm not referring to the old-fashioned type of teaching grammar by rote and separately from actual writing and speech but of a new grammar of speech and writing in the classroom as it occurs and with the aim of making one's voice clearer, more powerful and effective when putting one's case across to others. The old grammar schools tried to do this, indeed regarding it as a main aim that would eventually lead to a university education. But I think their methods were wrong when they concentrated on teaching grammar as a separate entity disconnected from the creative act of writing or debating. I always used to say 'we learn to swim by swimming; we learn to write by writing; and we learn to argue by arguing.''

Teaching pupils to write expressively and personally, using their five senses, is all well and good but it is quite a different thing to writing rationally in order to convince a reader to agree with a proposition or a point of view; and it is here where I think teachers of writing and debate need to develop ways of teaching

I hope the arguments and examples of pupils' writings I've supplied above show clearly enough how we encouraged the development of writing skills at Monkwick. As far as development of speech is concerned I cannot, obviously, provide examples that took place in my classroom fifty years ago. However, I am going to take samples from recorded speech I collected for some academic research I completed for the University of Lancaster in which I argue for the approaches we encouraged in classrooms at Monkwick in the 1960s. These aimed to encourage pupil participation in learning as opposed to rows and rows of pupils sitting silently while the teacher talked at them. As I said earlier, the Americans have argued: in any one classroom, whether it be a university lecture room or an infant class, a teacher is talking two thirds of the time, and for two thirds of that time s/he is giving his or her own opinions and providing facts while the thirty, or however many, pupils have to share the one third of the remaining verbal space between them. I wanted to be different at Monkwick so my classroom consisted of several tables around each one of which sat four or five pupils who were encouraged to learn by talking to each other about problems I set before them. This was the 1960s and several top educationists, including principally Douglas Barnes, argued that in the standard classroom with teacher out front doing most of the talking, pupils were not learning sufficiently or so well as they would do if they were in small peer groups, organising their own enquiries. It has been argued by many educationists that a "fundamental part of the learning process is the construction of meaning through language..." If this is so, then it should be asked how much talking actually goes on in classrooms and how much of this is spoken by teachers and how much by pupils. Is there genuine interaction between teachers and pupils when the teacher is principal actor in front of a class of say 30 pupils? Or will pupils learn more effectively when given the chance to interact with each other in small groups? Will it always be more conducive to learning if pupils have an authority figure supplying facts, explaining problems, analysing, and interpreting evidence, and drawing out and evaluating pupil responses? Or will pupils learn more from each other when they are attempting to do these things themselves in a peer group? Do pupils learn effectively, perhaps even more effectively when given the chance to interact with each other in small groups rather than with teacher as sole actor in front of the class?

In my research, at master's level, I tried to find answers to these questions by comparing the verbal responses of pupils in both teacher and pupil-led learning groups. Over a period of three years, I compared three groups of four pupils aged from eleven at the start to thirteen upwards at the end. The stimulus materials discussed in the groups were poems and prose extracts from literature selected for their relevance to the pupils' own experiences and abilities. The groups were mixed ability in as far as we could measure language, reading and writing on standardised tests available at the time. Two groups (A and B) had the piece read to them and were then given exactly the same amount of time (to the second) to discuss the text (copies of which were supplied to each individual). Group A was led by me as teacher and Group B controlled the discussion themselves. The discussions were audio recorded. This arrangement was switched each time the discussion groups met so that both groups (A) and (B) had equal amounts of time with and without the teacher. This procedure was followed throughout the duration of the research in order to build in a cross over effect for statistical purposes when speech and written test results were compared quantitatively. Although the control group (C) sat the subsequent written tests along with the other two groups they were never given time to discuss the literature as I needed to know whether discussion *of any sort* (teacher or pupil-led) led to better learning. So the control group simply had the poem or prose read to them and then dispersed. The recorded discussions of groups (A) and (B) were transcribed and from the subsequent printed evidence utterances were analysed at three second intervals. Two days after the reading and discussions all three groups were tested on their knowledge and understanding of the poem, story, or prose extract. The tests were set and marked anonymously by student teachers who had no prior knowledge as to which of the three groups the pupils belonged.

The research thus attempted to relate process to outcome, looking for connections between prior discussions and subsequent written answers as supplied in written tests. We were looking for evidence which might suggest that (a) some kind of learning had occurred because of previous verbal interaction, and (b) whether pupils learned more by being with a teacher or whether pupil-led learning in the absence of a teacher was equally or even more effective. Results of the subsequent written tests showed clearly that both groups who had participated in discussions scored significantly higher than the control group who did not have them. This is not at all surprising. But the results also showed that the teacher led groups did not score statistically significantly higher than the pupil-led groups in the post tests. So what were the differences between pupil-led and teacher-led teaching and learning? In a moment I'm going to quote a poem by Charles Causley, which was the subject for discussion for all three groups and you, the reader, will be asked to compare the effectiveness of the learning that is going on in each group. Obviously, this a one-off experiment that cannot be scientifically regarded as proving anything: the whole of the three-year project would have to be studied before any safe conclusions could be drawn and possibly backed by certain evidence. However, I thought it would be fun for the reader to see how one sample from the research project would lead to further questions as opposed to answers.

There follows a poem by Charles Causley which formed the subject matter for discussion by the teacher and pupil-led groups in one of the experiments. The reader is asked to read the poem carefully, perhaps more than once to ensure familiarity and hopefully pleasure. It was chosen as being relevant to and pleasurable for a group of 12-year-old boys and girls. After the poem I provide two transcripted extracts from the pupils' discussions, one being teacher-led and the other pupil-led. Again, the reader is asked to analyse the two discussions and evaluate them for their effectiveness in encouraging learning and pleasure in reading poetry.

<u>*By St. Thomas Water*</u>

By St. Thomas Water
Where the river is thin
We looked for a jam-jar
To catch the quick fish in.
Through St. Thomas churchyard
Jessie and I ran
The day we took the jam-pot
Off the dead man.

On the scuffed tombstone
The grey flowers fell,
Cracked was the water,
Silent the shell.
The snake for an emblem
Swirled on the slab.
Across the beach of sky the sun
Crawled like a crab.

'If we walk,' said Jessie,
'Seven times round,
We shall hear a dead man
Speaking under the ground.'
Round the stone we danced, we sang,
Watched the sun drop,
Laid our heads and listened
At the tomb-top.

Soft as the thunder
At the storm's start
I heard a voice as clear as blood,
Strong as the heart.
But what words were spoken
I can never say,
I shut my fingers round my head,
Drove them away.

'What are those letters, Jessie,
Cut so sharp and trim
All round this holy stone
With earth up to the brim?'
Jessie traced the letters
Black as coffin lead.
"HE IS NOT DEAD BUT SLEEPING"
Slowly she said.

I looked at Jessie,
Jessie looked at me,
And our eyes in wonder
Grew wide as the sea.
Past the green and bending stones
We fled hand in hand,
Silent through the tongues of grass
To the river strand.

By the creaking cypress
We moved as soft as smoke
For fear all the people
Underneath awoke.
Over all the sleepers
We darted light as snow
In case they opened up their eyes,
Called us from below.

Many a day has faltered
Into many a year
Since the dead awoke and spoke
And we could not hear.
Waiting in the cold grass
Under a crinkled bough,
Quiet stone, cautious stone
What do you tell me now?

Transcript

Teacher-led Group

Teacher reads second verse.

Julia: Oh, when they lifted the ummn the jar – jar – is it that a snake ran out of it or something

Like that? (Giggles)

T: Well that's a good – that's a good ummn go at it, there, Julia. Well done...Yes but I think

Ummnn?

Tom: I think the snake was on the tombstone – 'snake for an emblem'.

T: Yes...what's an emblem?

Tom: Well, a crest or something.

Robin: Yes.

T: *Uh huh (pause) It's not easy...'The snake for an emblem/Swirled on the slab'?...Does a Snake 'swirl'? (teacher's emphasis)*

Julia: *Oh no*

Jan: *Well...*

Gill: *Where does the snake come into it I'd like to know?*

Robin: *Maybe it was some sort of err – carved out of the stone and it was curled round?*

T: *Yes...? Possibly...?*

Julia: *Maybe it was a worm!*

(Laughter)

Tom: *No, it was a snake!*

Julia: *Yeah, I know, but it might have been a worm, they might have thought it was a snake.*

T: *Let's look back here. I think you might be...ummnn...confusing something here...*

(T. reads second verse again)

Later...

T: *Now, somebody suggested that the – Julia I think – that the pot has been smashed –*

Cracked.

Julia: *Yes, that was me.*

T: *Possibly...what would happen to the water?*

Tom: *It would spill out.*

Pupils: *Yes.*

T: *And it's spilled on the..?*

Tom: *Tombstone.*

T: *- and what does water do when it spills?*

Julia:	*Oh it goes like that, doesn't it. (She makes a swirling gesture).*
T:	*Yes.*
Pupils:	*Swirls!*
T:	*Swirls – like a snake.*
Pupils:	*Oh!*
T:	*So, is there really a snake there?*
Pupils:	*It's just water –*
T:	*It's just water…fine…now that you've got that…*

Transcript

Pupil-led

Jon:	*Ummnn they, they fear the ghosts are going to come up.*
Cath:	*Well, they've heard one.*
Jon:	*They've heard one, you know.*
Mel:	*Yeah.*
Cath:	*Yes – and just in case all the voices start err –*
Simon:	*- Because they're worried, they're moving 'soft as smoke' –*
Cath:	*- It's really frightening!*
Jon:	*Dancing about on tip toe, you know, all trying to get out!*
Cath:	*Yes, underneath 'We darted light as snow' – that's a good one as well.*
Pupil:	*Yeah.*

Jon: 'In case they opened up their eyes/Called us from below.'

Cath: Oh, that means –

Jon: – That means –

Cath: the earth would split, and the coffin would open and they would call them.

Pupil: Oh!

Jon: Yeah, or else the people just wake and would sort of entrance them and call them down.

Simon: Or they would be so frightened they couldn't resist it...

Cath: If you were in the graveyard –

Simon: – They must have been quite young because most people of our age don't normally believe in ghosts.

Cath: But if you're in a graveyard and it's at night and you're all alone it can get very scary –

Jon: – Yeah, I'm ever so scared at night.

Pupil: I've never been in a graveyard when it's been dark.

Jon: I have – it's 'orrible!

Cath: We had to walk through a graveyard this morning.

Jon: I do to have to get to my granny's...

Cath: well, they must have believed in the kind of poem about going seven times round the –

Jon: – Yeah.

Simon: There's one down Purley like that –

Cath: – Everybody's tried something once and if you're told not to do it you immediately want to do it.

Simon: I should think the children were told about this story before –

Pupil: *- Perhaps they heard someone saying about it –*

Cath: *- Perhaps they've got a granny who you know is very superstitious and said: 'If you walk seven times round a tomb' – they obviously heard the same line –*

Simon: *- Yeah, there's one down Purley about going twelve times round at twelve o' clock –*

Pupil: *- My legs would hurt –*

Simon: *- and they say a hand would come out and grab you in – take you –*

Jon: *- Cor, I must try that –*

Pupil: *- Have you ever tried that?*

Cath: *I wouldn't wake up in time...*

So how do these extracts from pupil-led and teacher-led discussion groups differ? First of all, I must make it clear that the extracts themselves cannot be compared strictly for any scientific or research purposes as they differ in time interval and strict subject matter (they speak of two different verses). However, I must point out to the reader that by and large they typify the kinds of learning behaviour that goes on in both teacher-led and pupil-led groups as witnessed by many long hours of analysis conducted over a three-year period in which several poems and prose extracts were discussed by the two groups. Also, every kind of test was given to the pupils initially in an effort to get an accurate balance of mixed ability in both groups; and of course the same teacher (myself) was the only one involved in the teaching. The first thing is to say that in the teacher - led group the teacher speaks almost exactly two thirds of the time, and this is in line with what the Americans have called their rule of two thirds: when the teacher is present the pupils have two thirds less time to contribute verbally. As I pointed out earlier, it has been argued by Douglas Barnes and others that a fundamental part of the learning process is the construction of meaning through language; and it can be argued that the pupils in the pupil-led learning group are at an advantage here, whilst the pupils with teacher are being directed towards *his* way of thinking worked out some time before and involving the meaning of the metaphor: "The snake for an emblem swirled on the slab". The pupils without a teacher sympathise with the children in the poem and relate similar experiences of their own when confronted by superstition and graveyards. The pupils in this group are having a good time and I regard their efforts as real learning in which they adopt a *hypothetical mode of speech* in which they respond to each other's contributions. They are enjoying the poem as they build through their questioning stance, they are achieving literary pleasure from a story well told; they are expressing sympathy; and they are telling their own stories, even their own jokes. What more could be asked when discussing a poem? Would it be true to say that whereas the teacher-led group is being *instructed,* however badly, the pupil-led are being *educated?* I think I have found an answer to this question by looking at the scores the pupils achieved in a post test that took place two days after their discussions. Here are the answers to a question and you, the reader, have to tell me which four pupils were in the teacher-led and which four were in the pupil-led. By the way, the tests were marked by student teachers none of whom knew which group the pupils were in.

The answers:

1. He could mean that the snake was cut into the rock because the man died of a snake bite.
2. By the snake he meant water that had come out of the jam pot and run or swirled on the slab or grave top.
3. 'The snake for an emblem swirled on the slab' is meaning that he dropped the pot, and the water ran like a snake on the slab.

4. 'The snake for an emblem' might mean he was killed by a snake or that was his family emblem.
5. The poet means when he said, 'The snake for an emblem swirled on the slab' that the water from the jampot was trickling away.
6. I think he is talking about the water, spilt from the vase and swirling around on the tomb.
7. Maybe because a snake has been carved on the grave.
8. I think he means there was a snake on it showing up.

It doesn't take a genius to recognise answers 2, 3, 5 and 6 were written by the teacher-led group and that 1, 4, 7 and 8 were written by members of the pupil-led group. The student teachers regarded answers that mentioned spilled water from the jar as being correct obviously agreed with the teacher that it was a metaphor symbolising the guilt of the children. So, is this how the exam system works? Pupils are told answers by a teacher and are rewarded when repeating those answers in a test.

No such problems with the pupil-led group who simply enjoyed themselves reading lines from the poem, interpreting them when they wanted, achieving group satisfaction, and, I believe, lots of pleasure as well of course as *educating* themselves. My argument has always been that pupils need greater freedom in the classroom to discover knowledge amongst themselves and that an extremely important *teaching skill* is to organise pupil-led or peer group learning. After all, we allow grown-ups to do this in their daily and professional work. That was why my classrooms were organised around small group learning groups, four or five to a table, rather than rows of chairs all pointing towards the teacher. This is not to take away any of the essential teaching skills required by teachers. Here, for instance in the example before us, there is a need for the teacher, when summarising, to inform the whole class of the meaning of metaphor and his own explanation of the particular one where the poet writes: "The snake for an emblem/Swirled on the slab." And of course listen to any alternatives that may disagree with his interpretation!

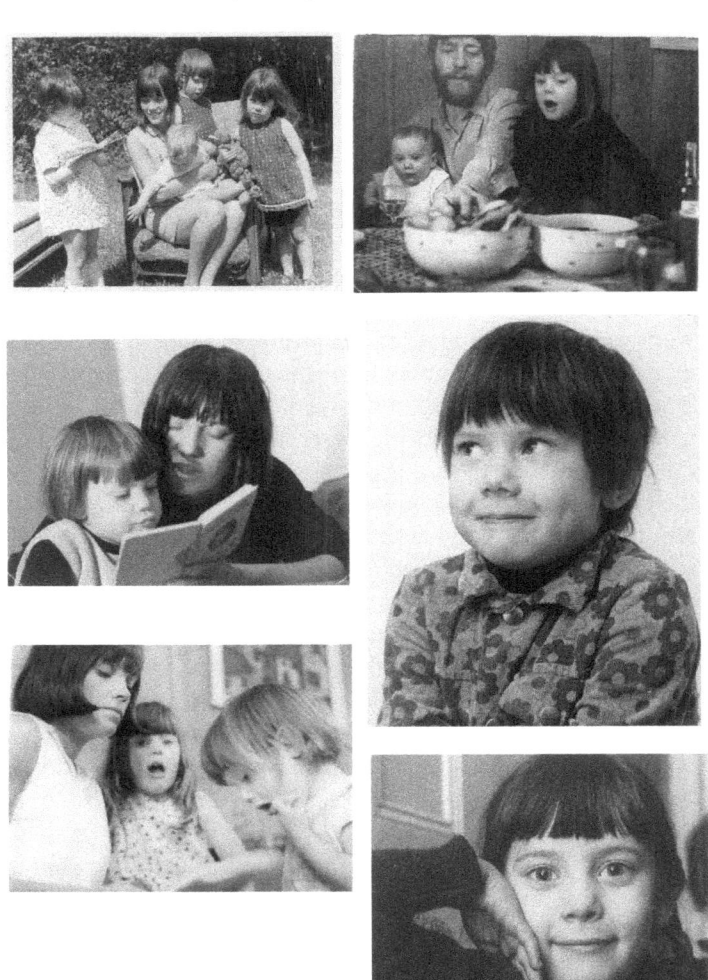

Barbara and the children

Early marriage

While my teaching progressed Barbara was being a mother to our three children and running the home as a typical housewife. We recognised Barbara's intellectual ability of course – obvious to anyone conversing with her – and she attended various evening classes including Russian, woodwork, and drama – but none of us had any idea that she had this tremendous capacity for hard work at such a deep intellectual level (summarized in the earlier quotation about the professional achievements that followed).

In that first ten years we did the typical things that most married couples did in the early sixties. We liked visits to the pub with friends, read books avidly, watched films and met up with some of my fellow teachers at various social occasions. We loved the songs of Bob Dylan who, incidentally, is exactly the same age as Barbara. She was kept busy with the three children who, at one stage early on were all aged below three years! It was a time when there were no disposable nappies, so we were kept busy. Barbara got a job working in a nursery and she met up with mothers whose husbands taught at the University of Essex. So, our intellectual life was continuously stimulated and the three children were all doing well at school.

Our really big breakthrough came when we all moved temporarily to Birmingham where I took a year's advanced course in education. We all moved up there and Barbara was lucky enough to attend an evening class that taught the first 'A' level course in psychology. That was it!

All would change now! Barbara loved the work and obtained an 'A' grade. This was the beginning of her towering collection of qualifications and international awards. From Birmingham the family moved to Reading where I had obtained a post as lecturer in educational studies at Bulmershe College of Higher Education and Barbara began a degree course in Psychology at Reading University. Barbara obtained a first class honours degree and I was lucky enough to have sufficient free time to look after the kids. This situation continued for a further few years while Barbara obtained her Ph.D. while working at the Maudsley Hospital. This involved her travelling up to London each day, so I took on care of the house and children from breakfast to dinner: a genuine house husband! I was not happy lecturing: to be honest I much preferred school teaching, but this was no longer possible.

This was a significant time in our lives together and as a family. It was the beginning of Barbara's career, which has continued to flourish for fifty years and the start of an era in which I took on a more caring family role while my career took second place to Barbara's. I didn't mind this at all, and I was able to help Barbara with her writing by taking on editorial and proof reading roles that have been of significant support in the publication of her work, both in terms of the enormous number of books she has published and her hundreds of research publications. This secondary role also enabled me to start a career in publishing which proved to be very successful, leading to the setting up of my own company which I eventually sold after thirteen profitable years enabling me to travel internationally often accompanying Barbara: she lecturing at workshops while I sold test publications. To give you an idea of the extent of these travels, as part of them Barbara visited and stayed in 49 of the USA's fifty states! My teaching career was over, and I had been able to take early retirement from lecturing at Bulmershe College. Barbara and I continued to be a very close professional team as well as being in a loving marriage which continues to this day now that we are both in our eighties! I want to stress that we have come to the whole point of this book: to emphasise that it is possible for a husband to take on a secondary role when it comes to earning a living; and to take on the role of housekeeper, principal carer of children, and house administrator. I ask again: "Can I be regarded as a Modern Man?"

Barbara obtained a post as a clinical psychologist working with brain injured patients at Rivermead Rehabilitation Centre (RRC) in Oxford. She loved this work and was extremely happy there: her work formed the basis of her expertise in brain injury rehabilitation that informed her later years.

One extraordinary event took place at Barbara's workplace at Rivermead and is worth noting for what it tells us about her bravery and political commitment to the National Health Service. I think it best if I get her to describe the event in her own words, taken from her book "The Story of a Clinical Psychologist" (Routledge, 2020).

"Life was progressing well, I was publishing, attending conferences, treating patients, and giving lectures when we realised RRC was in trouble. The health authority wanted to close RRC to save money. A meeting was called and one of the senior managers said that if a facility was to close there had to be a three-month consultation period but this could be avoided as the health authority would say they were temporarily closing the centre and then after three months they would really close it! Many of the RRC staff were shocked at this deception and decided to try to reverse the decision. I wrote to everyone I knew in the world and asked if they would write a letter to the Oxfordshire Health Authority to say how important was RRC and that it should be saved. This happened and the authority was surprised at our abundant support but decided not to change their minds. A date was set for builders to come in and start demolition. A small group of us met to decide our next steps and concluded we had no choice but to occupy the centre, that is to say we would take over the running of the centre and prevent any builders coming in. I agreed to chair the occupation committee. There were others just as capable, but many feared they would lose their jobs if too closely allied to the occupation. I had little fear partly because this is not in my nature and partly because at that time clinical psychologists were in short supply and there were plenty of

jobs available. We were all committed to the belief that patient care would not suffer, we would allow no alcohol on the premises and do everything legally. Occupation was, at that time anyway, legal. We had to inform the police and put up a symbolic rope across the entrance plus a notice saying this was a legal occupation. We also had to have people at the gate at all times. We could not tell everyone in the centre as we knew that not all thought we were doing the right thing and if the authority was informed, we would be prevented from putting up the notice and the rope. We certainly could not tell the consultant as she would prevent it. I had a trainee with me at the time and she helped to write and laminate the notice. I wondered if I should be asking her to do this but reasoned that if she was going to work in the NHS, she should learn how to fight for it.

The day came to start the occupation, it was shortly before Christmas, and we knew that the consultant would be out for lunch with her secretary so we decided that was the time to put up the symbolic rope and the notice. The rope and notice were installed, the police were informed; we had a rota of people willing to be at the gate. This included Mick who did his regular shifts there. The press was informed and gave us good coverage. We had a brazier to keep us warm and to cook the potatoes that local farmers left for us. Many people going past in their cars sounded their horns to show their support. The police were less enthusiastic and, at first, did not recognise the legality of what we were doing. However, we had a lawyer advising the team and he contacted the police to say that if they thought what we were doing was illegal they needed to change their lawyers. The police attitude changed a little, but it was clear they did not like what we were doing. Most of the city did seem to approve though and the Oxford students even organized a march in support.

We sent a letter to the health authority saying we requested a three-month consultation period as was our legal right. Fortunately, a new chief executive had recently been appointed to the health authority and this was the first major problem he had to deal with. Not only that but he was sympathetic to our views. It took 18 days before we received a letter from this man saying he agreed to a three-month consultation period. The occupation was called off and life returned to normal. Nobody lost their jobs. And Mick could stop pretending he was Che Guevarra! I was congratulated and received offers of other posts. As far as I know this was the only successful occupation of an NHS facility."

(The Story of a Clinical Neuropsychologist, Barbara A. Wilson, Routledge2020)

Barbara

Author's note: I'd just like to add here that all the time Barbara was pursuing her illustrious career she steadfastly remained a caring and unselfish mother and partner. I am not just a modern man – I'm a lucky one!

Mick carries on

Another extraordinary and quite horrific incident occurred when I attended a conference in Washington DC when representing my publishing company, Thames Valley Test Co. (printed with permission from Routledge).

"The year was 2000 and it was only weeks since our beloved oldest child, Sarah, had died in the white water rafting accident in Peru. For some time prior to the accident, I had been committed to exhibiting some of Thames Valley Test Company's products at a conference in Washington D.C., USA. I had to go: a table had been booked, various items from stock had been delivered, some US agents were expecting me to be there; and of course, I would be able to take orders from conference delegates.

The conference lasted for a couple of days and then it was time to get my flight back to England, at about 6.00 p.m. Passengers assembled at the allotted terminal expecting to be called for boarding when an announcement was made to the effect that the flight had to be delayed because of a faulty door on the plane which could not be locked shut. OK, these things happen, so maybe we'll be delayed by an hour or two until either the door is fixed or a spare one is found, or another plane can take us. I was carrying my desktop computer – quite heavy in those days twenty years ago - and a carry-on case. It was difficult to find a seat so I wandered around and eventually found floor space, holding on to computer and case not having anywhere to leave them. Several others were finding places to rest on the floor while the lucky ones who came earlier had the few seats that were around.

We waited and waited and waited as the clock got nearer to 10 o'clock. As usual there was no news from any officials and passengers were getting restless. In particular, there breakfast in a street café was even grimmer next morning. I was in a desperately unhappy neighbourhood of lost souls with seemingly nothing to live for. I don't think I've ever felt so depressed!

At the court I didn't understand what was going on. I'd had to wait for about an hour before I was called, and it was arranged that I would have to come back to the States sometime in the future to face judgement in a proper court proceeding. As I left the courtroom, I heard some footsteps approaching from behind quite rapidly, felt a hand on my shoulder and a pleasant looking guy smiled at me, explained that he was a defence attorney and would I like him to take on my case. I almost cried at hearing this pleasant, sympathetic voice and agreed that he should defend me. I seemed to have a friend who would genuinely listen and would perhaps believe my story! We exchanged addresses and emails and I felt for the first time that justice could evolve. I had heard about 'ambulance chasers': attorneys who chase down accident victims even before they get to hospital and how dubious the system is but this guy was the only person I could hold onto. Who else was there to fight my corner?

I made my way to the airport and was lucky enough to be able to get on to a flight to London that was leaving within the hour. On the plane I recognised some of the people who had not been able to get on the second flight last night. One of them was the bearded guy who had behaved so abominably. Being the year 2000 there were very few beards worn that year, they didn't become fashionable until about 2010, I think. Well, there seemed to be only the two of us with beards.

At home and at work my lifeline turned out to be the attorney: he was caring about me, sympathetic and very sorry for our loss of Sarah. He kept in touch regularly by phone and email and told me he was working especially on my state of mind at not being able to get home at a time when our family needed to grieve together. Time dragged on for several weeks and I remained permanently anxious. Of course I discussed the issues with a number of friends, none of whom could get past their ignorance of the way justice proceeded in the USA. However, one very important point was raised by our graphic designer who stated that there must have been cameras in such a sensitive area as the boarding terminal and we should ask for them to be seen as part of a properly thorough investigation. This was passed on to the attorney who still argued for a sympathetic appreciation of my state of mind at that time of night, having missed two flights and needing to get back to a grieving family. The upshot was that I sent a full coverage of Sarah's death in the white-water accident that had appeared in the local newspaper: there were photos of her, the raging river in which she died, and pictures of Barbara and me mourning. It was an impressive coverage and very, very sad.

Were these final efforts going to work on the American Prosecutor, who himself would, apparently, have to persuade the American police force to drop the case? A few days later I got a phone call from the attorney to say the case against me had been dropped. I could tell he was delighted, and I was greatly relieved. Which argument worked on the Prosecutor? The sentimental one or the properly legal one? I'll never know but I'm left with bewilderment at the mysterious ways American justice seems to work. My impression is that if the American police want to get you, they will. They are, as they say, a law unto themselves.

About a week later I got a bill for a thousand dollars from the attorney. Much later on, and to this day, I wonder whether the two policemen who got me to the ground were in fact asked to arrest the elderly bearded guy who was causing so much harm by insulting the American Nation? Was I mistakenly picked out? The two policemen could have felt they'd got their man and he was sure going to suffer. Certainly, the policemen seemed to come from nowhere. They appeared on the scene and immediately arrested me."

("Reaching for Fulfilment as a Woman in Science, Barbara A. Wilson, Routledge, 2021)

I wrote that account and added it to Barbara's book at a time when the whole world was still reeling from the killing of George Floyd in the USA by policemen in such an atrocious, sadistic, manner during a violent arrest. I keep thinking of all those black guys who get arrested in the USA, and here in the UK. How much worse it is for them, how they have to fight to save their lives, to escape arrest within a system where they have no means of obtaining justice, how so many of them are killed! My release makes me and indeed our whole family part of racism in the sense that we, being white, can use a system to protect our innocence; we have the financial means to pay for attorneys, we can talk to witnesses; we can write letters to powerful people explaining our position, call upon witnesses, refer to newspaper articles as we did. In other words, we are part of a system that is largely denied to black people and that is why black lives matter and not white lives: white lives are safe enough. We are already cared for and the world must be changed so *all* of us, white and black, are cared for; we must all have a *fair* chance to protect our innocence.

Just to complete my story in Washington, I was able to get a young American woman to write a witness account, which I forwarded to my attorney, and I include below. This account didn't seem to carry weight with the prosecutor. I have not included the young woman's name at her request as she remains somewhat afraid of upsetting the American police.

"Witness account of Michael Wilson's Arrest
I was a witness to Michael Wilson's arrest around midnight on August 8. Many others and I were appalled at how this arrest was conducted and shocked that it ever took place.

There were many of us scheduled to fly out on August 7th. Due to mechanical problems with the plane, the Airline told everyone around midnight that the flight was cancelled, and we were told to line up to try and book on other flights going to Europe around midnight or soon after. Mind you, many people had been waiting in the airport for over 7 hours and people were getting restless and upset as they stood in line. While waiting in line, I saw Michael Wilson and he was waiting patiently and had a calm demeanor under the circumstances.

After waiting in line for approximately 45 minutes, I noticed 3 police officers coming round to the area. Next, the flight clerk announced that there were no more bookings on any other European flights and that we would have to go to the main terminal to get hotel vouchers and on to new flights. At this point people all around started to yell out comments of anger towards the Airline representatives. One of the angriest people was a man with a British accent that was really mad and making a scene. This person was not Michael Wilson. Before the yelling and screaming got out of hand, I noticed the police giving people warnings. At this time, Michael Wilson was not one of them. After the Airline representative got off the loudspeaker, I noticed Michael Wilson going up to the representative's desk and ask a question with his hand to his ear. I don't know what exactly was said, but as he backed up, he bumped into the police officer. Within seconds, Michael had three officers pushing him back and putting handcuffs around his wrists. As they were pushing him, Michael's leg got caught up in the straps of my duffle bag. I was trying to free up my bag when the police told me to back off. I was dumbfounded at the overreaction the police took out on Michael. I was in shock to see them treat him as though he was resisting arrest. I witnessed this situation and believe that Michael Wilson did not deserve this kind of treatment in our great country, The United States of America.

Right away I started to question why the officers treated Michal Wilson the way they did. I came up with two possible reasons.

    1. Maybe the officer made a mistake and thought Michael Wilson was the other British man who was outraged and yelling out loud (that I mentioned earlier).

> 2. *Maybe the officers wanted to set an example out of Michael who was trying to ask a question of the airline representative.*
>
> *Minutes after the police escorted Michael out, there were many people standing around with disbelief. About a dozen of us were discussing how we should write letters of some kind to help Michael out. The only problem was we didn't know where or who to send them to. The next day we ran into Michael at the airport and offered to support him in any way possible. This is why I am writing this witness account. I believe that what happened to Michael was an injustice, and I would hope that justice will prevail in this case."*
>
> *(Name withheld owing to continued fear of police reaction)*

As I explained initially, this book would be based on half a century of my life, from childhood at the beginning of the Second World War in 1939, when I was four year's old, until the last day of the millennium, 2000, when I was 65. Skipping a few years both Barbara and I, and our son and two daughters, all moved from Reading back to Suffolk in 1990. Barbara was employed by the Medical Research Council, in Cambridge, I ran the publishing business from home, and Sarah, our eldest worked at home with me at Thames Valley Test Company. Sarah had also married Gez and they both lived with us in a small hamlet named Flempton. Our house was originally four tiny, terraced thatched cottages made into one long thatched building. Our daughter Anna, now divorced from her first husband Paul, lived with her two daughters in a nearby village, and Matthew, our son, got married to a lovely Chilean woman who was a brilliant wine maker and they lived together in Chile, Matthew being self-employed there as a food and wine photographer.

We were a happy and hardworking family for the next ten years although some major changes took place in our circumstances. For a start, I sold the business to a Dutch company and became a manager for them; both Sarah and Anna's marriages broke up, particularly bad for Sarah who did not want the separation from Gez. Anna then became single for several years until she at last met a wonderful man, Michael. Together they have built up a most successful marriage and splendid home. Matthew and Andrea in Chile have two beautiful sons; Andrea was voted best wine maker in Chile – the first woman to receive this honour - and Matthew has won several international photography competitions. Rosie, our oldest granddaughter is in a very happy gay relationship with Hope and they live only a few miles away with their two children, Amélie and Conroy. Our other granddaughter Francesca is also in a very strong partnership with Jack, living quite close to Rosie, so we see quite a bit of the extended family apart from Matthew's family living so far away in Chile.

In the year 2000, after Sarah and Gez got divorced, Sarah decided she would give up her work and travel back to Peru to continue her mountain biking and occasional journalism. As part of her adventures she chose to do some white water rafting in the Cotahuasi Canyon in Peru. Most people would think that the Grand Canyon of Arizona is the deepest valley in the world but they are wrong. It is about 1737 metres deep, just over a mile. The deepest valley in the world is the Cotahuasi Canyon with a depth of about 3,354 metres.

Sarah

Our Search For Sarah

It is time now to complete this book of mine. It has been my intention all along to end it at the start of the new millennium when Sarah, our lovely eldest child, met her death in a white-water rafting accident in the Cotahuasi Valley in Peru. Both Barbara and I want to go no further than end with a tribute to Sarah who all the family agree was a special individual whose tragic loss has been so unbearable. I begin by quoting from Barbara's journal of that search, first published in "First Year, Worst Year" by John Wiley & Sons, Ltd., in 2004)

Crossing a bridge

"I slept for several hours on and off in the van, perhaps because of the altitude. For much of the time we were travelling at around 5000 metres (16,400 feet). We arrived at the hostel in Cotahuasi town exactly 12 hours after leaving Arequipa. This was the same hostel the five of us stayed in last year, with the flooded courtyard.

There was no flooding this time. The owner remembered us and was friendly and welcoming. The food was better than last year because Raoul cooked it. We slept well.

The weather on the following day was glorious, bright, crisp and clear showing the magnificent mountains nearby at their best. While Pepé, Edwin and Raoul were loading the van, Mick and I set off for a quick walk around the town, which still seemed in a time warp. We filmed the blacksmith shoeing a horse (a good scene), but we also saw a little girl, possibly aged about eight years, who was looking after two drunken or drugged parents (not a good scene). Earlier, Mick had seen the man lying with his back against a wall, with his hat pulled down over his eyes – looking like a scene out of a Clint Eastwood film. The child looked at Mick with embarrassment as she vainly pulled at her father's sleeve. Mick turned away in respect for the little girl. Later we were to talk about this incident and Mick compared the wonderfully happy but short life of Sarah with what must be going on in the little girl's life. We knew that Sarah had had an almost idyllic childhood in comparison and wondered what lay in store for the little girl.

We set off to collect the mules and donkeys at a lower level in the valley. There was a considerable amount of unloading of the van and loading of the pack animals, so we went off for a walk. Pepé had hired a father and son to look after the animals. There were three donkeys, which carried most of the luggage, tents and provisions plus two mules which carried a few things and one horse which did not carry anything (the load distribution did not seem fair). At first, we followed the same track that we had taken last year. By 1 pm we were near the Sipia falls, close to the place where we held last year's ceremony. We did not feel the need to go to the falls again so pushed on.

Mick after dipping into the river

The next part of the trek, part of an old Inca trail, was steep so Pepé suggested we ride. I was given the horse and Mick one of the mules. After 20 minutes Mick said he wanted to walk as he did not feel in control. I was enjoying the ride and felt the horse was probably more sure-footed than me on the steep, shale-like, path. Mick is always more nervous of animals than me. He said he was petrified! He walked the rest of the way while I did a mixture of walking and riding. I had to dismount for the steep downhill parts and rode going uphill. Eventually, however, I just walked as I needed to stretch my legs.

The scenery was spectacular with wonderful mountains, colours, and shapes. I found it extraordinarily beautiful, the most beautiful scenery I had ever seen. I know Sarah would have loved it and I was glad she had experienced such beauty before she died. On the other hand, neither she nor I would have known about this place if she had not gone on the trip and, of course, I would prefer never to have seen this beauty if it meant having Sarah back. We reached Chaupo, our camping spot, at 3.50 pm. It was an oasis of green in the rocky surroundings. The place was a farm and

Sarah had stayed there too on her way to the rafting part of the trip.

Mick in the canyon

The animals had a good drink in a stream and Pepé talked about the accident. He said that Sarah was conscious at first and had looked directly at him from the water as it swept her past him. She was the last of the five to come out of the 'hole'. The raft had not turned over as we had thought but had upended, so the guide had remained on the raft. We had always wondered why he did not go in the water too. So, five people went in the water and Sarah was the last to emerge from this whirlpool-type place. Pepé thought she might have broken her neck just as we were told at the memorial service. At first she was choking and in the correct position but soon after there was another rapid. When she emerged from that she was completely lifeless and just tossed about. Pepé followed her by boat, and on foot, for about 20 minutes but she was floating very very quickly. It was so, so sad. My poor, lovely, beautiful girl. I wanted her back so very much.

Where the raft went in

We walked to the tents that had been pitched in a field owned by the farmer. Again, it was so beautiful there with the steep mountains, the lush meadow, the tethered pack animals and the farmer's cows and dogs. Our animals had a good feed from the tall grass around. Earlier in the day we had seen a herd of llamas. They looked as if they had been dyed as their coats were a mixture of rust and white. However, Pepé told us these were old Inca colours and quite natural. We had seen lots of llamas grazing over the past two days, but this morning's group were being herded. We had also seen an eagle and several hawks but very few people and no tourists of course. Raoul provided a good meal that we ate under the stars. We had soup, beef curry and rice together with a bottle of Chilean wine. We went to bed surrounded by the tethered donkeys, mules, horses, cows and sheep.

On May 29th, we enjoyed a breakfast of hot French toast. Our 'showers' were pretty basic; we were given a basin of water each just like in Mali. We trudged across the field to find a toilet spot and became covered in burrs so spent ages de-burring ourselves. I was not completely *successful and kept finding burrs for days afterwards. Some even turned up back in England. Pepé, Mick and I left at 8.30. I found a stick that helped me up and down the steep parts of the trail. Some of the paths were tricky being shingle and shale on precipitous cliffs and narrow paths so we had to go very slowly in some places.*

Last picture of Sarah

At this point I am presenting Sarah's own diary of the last five days of her life before the fatal day of the 12th of May. She describes the scenery that has been covered in this final chapter. The diary was among her belongings, and I found it extremely painful to read – just once and then it was put away until now, when I begin typing from her handwritten script…"
Sarah wrote:

<u>*Sunday 7th May*</u>

"Woke up early, toothache easier. Stuff all ready – checked out but took key with me! No problems with flight except got

there early boring wait with no café. Met at Arequipa by Cachimira(?), went to hotel which is very nice. Met rest of group briefly and went straight for tour of monastery – v. beautiful in places. Ate wonderful meal – excellent cow's heart and local freshwater shrimp. Some people went for siesta, but others went to shops (no whiskey!). On Place des Armes, local girls went crazy for gringo men. Chris (good-looking one) kept getting his photo taken. Group seems really nice. Paul turned up 7.30, six of us went for food and beer at German pub. All the guides turned up and stayed late, but us punters went back for an early night.

<u>Monday 8th May</u>

6.00 start – 7.00 departure. Straight to airport for Sue's luggage. Hung around for a while, nearly bought cheap local rum but found whiskey just in time. Bus is brand new and <u>really</u> luxurious – all it needs is a toilet and Paul coming round with tea and biscuits on a tray. First half (distance-wise) is on easy tarmac – then last half on terrible roads but absolutely <u>awesome</u> scenery. Frequently changing, started as desert, boulder fields…then climbed high into mountains – dramatic, snowy peaks. Saw vicuna (3 groups), a rabbit-like animal called a vicachi (?), and, late in the day, a bobcat. V. rare to see these – had large, bushy, stripy tail. Roadworks at one point due to landslide, took advantage of break to have lunch. Other truck coming up whilst diggers throwing rocks down. Max shouted down 'Fucking idiots' (in Spanish). They reached us and got out carrying huge gun. Said it was for shooting chinchillas but looked like it was for show. Chris and Geoff suffered badly from altitude sickness (the 2 smokers!) – Geoff especially looked really ill. I felt fine. Reached Cotahuasi late – desperate to find somewhere to eat. Hostel not too bad – but wouldn't risk the bed clothes! Found little dive to eat in. OK, good hot sauce. Bit of a shock for some of the others though.

Tuesday 9th May

Drove out of town for 1 hour to end of road. Pretty exciting drive – had to get out once. Most walked last bit – just Paul, Max, Sue and I stayed in. Some great views down the canyon. Paul and 2 Pepés took trekkers off, others stayed to load mules. Stunning scenery – bit like Arizona. Amazing red colours. Trekked 2 hours to Sepia falls – real vertigo territory. Bathed, ate lunch, got braver about approaching edge. Set off 2 hrs. later for 3 hour trek – Geoff on a mission – sprinted off into distance. Quite a climb, v. narrow with off cumber path on scree slope – scary. Took it easy at back – got to campsite around 4 pm. Waterfall disappointing – managed a bit of a wash. Discovered 2 mules missing – Geoff and Chris's gear has gone, plus some food (all the chocolate!). Reme set off back along route to look for them. Ate mild curry, drank a lot of Chilean red (late start tomorrow), told dirty jokes (especially Max and Nick).

Wednesday 10th May

No sign of mules. We set off – leaving muleteers to wait for Reme. 2 hours trek – through cactus fields – not so much climbing as yesterday but v. narrow, single track. Would be v. technical on a mountain bike. Got to river at 11.15 – that white-water noise will be our backing track for next 6 days. Camp on beach, but bedspaces are in short supply. Guys have found a donkey-field but it's a bit of a scramble to get to. Had lunch, tried bathing but the river is freezing. Also, they were right – the rapids are "continuous" Had a siesta – mules very late. Eventually turn up at 3.00 pm., with <u>most</u> of missing stuff, but no food or safety ropes. Paul will leave, with Reme – local muleteer leader to find the thief. (Mules were stolen (!) at start of trek, thief had buried stuff along route to his house. Reme tracked mules back to house, which was locked.) We will stay here – if Paul is back by 12.00 tomorrow we will set off in afternoon. Evening – some people walked to village but couldn't get wine – they will *bring it tomorrow. I went with Sue, Peter, Martin and Cashimira to hot springs. About 1 km. walk – at a real fast pace along beach, small pool of warm water. Had a wonderful bath, then got hot and sweaty walking back in the dark. Ate, had a little whiskey. More bad, filthy jokes.*

Thursday 11th May

Slept till 7.00 (a lie-in) – could have slept longer, but too worried I would miss breakfast! 2 big bowls porridge later. Set off for another session at hot springs with Pepe Lopez, Chris, Nick, Geoff and Sue. Shaved my legs! And Nick had a shave. Max arrived too late to take pictures. Came back, sunbathed for a couple of hours. Edgar arrived back with mule and all the gear except the food – what a hero! Paul has gone to Cotahuasi to buy more food – we will leave tomorrow. In the meantime, it is time for swimming/rescue lesson. Feeling very nervous, but it turns out quite easy. In the end we all go in, although Sue and I are the only ones sensible enough to wear wetsuits. Max nearly didn't go in, but got so much abuse he was forced to, and quite enjoyed it after all."

Sarah (The Story of a Clinical Neuropsychologist, Barbara A. Wilson, Routledge 2020)

Back to Barbara's diary

"We saw the accident site first from above. Pepé told us that two mules had been stolen from the trip with Sarah, and that one of these had been carrying all the safety gear so the group had to wait two days for replacement safety gear. He said that if the gear had arrived one day later, the whole trip would have been aborted. That made us feel very bad. Just one more day and they would never have started that wretched rafting! We indulged in more "if onlys" then. "If only the gear had arrived one day later." or "If only the gear had not been stolen and they had left two days earlier, the river would not have been so high, and they might never have been upended." It seemed as if everything had conspired against Sarah.

Before reaching the place where we could see the accident site, we had walked through the cactus forest where Max Milligan had taken a picture of the group striking funny poses among the cacti. This was also the spot where the last known photograph of Sarah was taken – the one where she looked so happy. Pepé took a photograph of Mick and me in the same spot. I wept there and wept when we saw the river from above. We reached the riverbank at 1.30 and from then on, we kept stopping and starting for Mick to film everything and for Pepé to give us the narrative on film. "This is where the boat got stuck". "This is where they were all swimming". "This is where Sarah was floating down with no control going over the other rapid". "This is where I last saw her". "This is where we think she is," and so on.

I was appalled that anyone could go into this terrible, churning water with so many rocks to be injured by. Yet Pepé said that the water was less fierce this year. It was now considered a grade 4 whereas last year it was a grade 5. How could the organisers have let people go in and how could the people agree? If I had been Sarah, I would have flatly refused to enter the water.

Throughout the day we had seen only one man with three

donkeys, two men with a mule and some donkeys and two lone men hiking. The place was truly remote and isolated. We had found the trekking physically demanding and emotionally painful even though part of us appreciated the beauty and wildness of this part of the Peruvian Andes. We reached the camp site that was in a beautiful valley just below the scene of the accident, feeling tired. We enjoyed a salad, coca cola and pineapple juice and watched four Torrent ducks playing and swimming in the raging waters of the river. Pepé said it was unusual to see two pairs of these birds together and not common to see even one pair. We watched these fragile birds for a long time, enjoying their ability to swim against the turbulent waters. We felt they were a sign from Sarah, saying, "Be happy." Even though in my heart I did not believe in such signs, we watched out for them during the trip. Pepé believed in such signs and Mick said the birds were a sign for him that Sarah was in this place. At the very least, these playful, entertaining birds seemed like a symbol of hope. We decided to have the ceremony just above this spot the next day. Before dinner we walked among the Inca and pre-Inca ruins nearby. There were impressive acres of walled terraces. We could feel the spirit of these old civilisations and felt it was a good place for Sarah to be. If she had to die then she would have appreciated resting forever in this remote, wild, beautiful valley with the spirits of the Incas all around. That night we saw the Southern Cross above the river. This is Mick's favourite constellation. Again, it seemed to be another sign that Sarah was there, especially when we saw a shooting star flash in front of the four points of the cross. It was a brilliant night lit by stars we felt we could touch. They would shine down on Sarah night after night forever. (First Year, Worst Year, Barbara A. Wilson, John Wiley & Sons, 2004)

Mick again

Two years later I wrote the following poem that was inspired by this starry night by the river. I also include an interesting footnote to the occasion of the writing.

I can talk to you Sarah
Although you're not here
I know where you were
When you were last seen
Face down in the water.

Dead stones as if amazed watching
Your progress to a fast death.

You always wanted the passion of speed and grace
And mindlessness
As in a supreme sport
Though in fact you were
Uncoordinated to be truthful.

You got what you always wanted
In that last journey,
Fast, furious, delirious.
Supremely sporting could one say?

A year later
We take our time
In the river valley
Filled with life and growth.

At night it has the brightest stars
You will ever see!

> Are you watching
> My lovely daughter
> Now that you are part of this valley,
> This land, this continent, this revolving planet?
>
> Do you feel the speed
> Of the universe?
>
> Look, my star is moving with all the others!
> Faster than anything!

I had just completed this poem late on Thursday, the 16th of October and went out into the garden to look at the stars. Almost immediately a shooting star shot rapidly across the low sky from east to west. It was not one of those feint stars high above, like a scratch on a blackboard but a reddish and very obvious slash, almost comet-like, leaving a fading trace in its wake. I went back into the house. Fifteen minutes later I said to myself, 'I'll go into the garden again and if I see another shooting star I'll take is as a sign' (Even though I am a non-believer in such things). As I opened the door, and before I got out into the garden, another star, even brighter than the first shot across the sky from west to east.)

Barbara's diary continues

"In the morning Mick picked a safe place in the river to bathe. The water was icy cold and took his breath away. He thought of Sarah's body being trapped, maybe a couple of hundred metres higher up the valley and wondered whether any atom of her was in the water in which he bathed.

Mick and I set off with Pepé the next morning. We took the CD memorial tape, the Walkman and speakers together with some "presents" to throw into the river for Sarah. The place we decided to hold the ceremony was the spot where Sarah was presumed to be dead or at least unconscious before being pulled down into the depths. Pepé moved away, Mick set up the speakers on some rocks and we began.

Our ceremony for Sarah

First, I told her about the memorial service in October and threw in a copy of the programme. Before we played the first song, Dylan's "Don't think twice it's all right", I said that Matthew had chosen the songs for the memorial service. We were overcome and held each other, both of us were crying. I then told Sarah about a book I had just read called "It's not just the bike" by Lance Armstrong, the American cyclist who overcame cancer and won the Tour de France on three occasions. I knew Sarah would have liked the book, so I threw my copy into the river for her. We played song number two beginning "I always flirt with death". A copy of Anna's speech was thrown in next. I told Sarah that this was the best speech of the service. I read the last paragraph aloud before throwing it in the river. The third song, "Just like Fred Astaire" came next. Simon, Jo, Cameron and Molly had given us a card and a photograph to go into the river so these went in along with a short piece I had written for The Compassionate Friends Newsletter.

"I wish I were a fisherman" was played and then Mick made a little speech for Sarah. He threw in a pen from his publishing company where Sarah had worked for 14 years and a postcard of Heron Island where Sarah had always wanted to go. Finally, we played the song I now always associate with Sarah "Forever Young", again by Dylan. During the ceremony there was one lonely swallow flying above and one beautiful yellow butterfly skimming the water. Once again, these appeared to be signs that Sarah was there and at peace. Pepé came up and hugged us saying how sorry he was. We felt it had been a good service but emotionally exhausting.

Pepé and Barbara in a mild tributary

By this time the others had loaded up the animals and we left. The first part of the route was fairly easy, but then we had to wade across a fast-flowing stream. Pepé took our backpacks across first, then he led me and then Mick. It was not easy finding our footing and keeping upright. This was only a stream, yet we were made aware of the power of the water. Before lunch, Pepé took us into the house of a farmer he knew. The farm was by the riverbank. There had been a landslide there 20 days earlier and the farmer had lost land and fruit trees. He gave us wine and made us welcome. I realised he was talking, in Spanish, to Pepé about Sarah. Of course, everyone along the river knew about her and about the reward for her body. As we left, he said in Spanish, "You are welcome here at any time". I cried at this kindness.

Next morning, Mick wanted to film and take photographs. We walked until noon with a few brief stops. We had crossed the most frightening path – a ridge a few inches wide across a steep, shale slope. This was the path I had travelled on horseback on the way out. This time we walked across with Pepé, one at a time. I thought, "Don't think about the drop, just go slowly, just put one foot in front of the other". It is a good thing I am not of a nervous disposition as this particular path would have made me very nervous.

Back in Cotahuasi town, we returned to the Hostal Chavez. We phoned Anna. She was pleased to hear from us. I think people at home had been anxious about the trip. They were not sure we would cope.

Just before 5 pm we set off with the owner of the hostel, his wife and daughter to drive to the thermal baths. Sarah had been there in May 2000, and we had all been there the year before, in 2001, when Rosie had been the centre of attention. If white tourists were unusual, white children were particularly unusual. We swam there although the high temperature made it difficult to swim for very long.

On Friday June 1st we set off for the long journey back to Arequipa. We had breakfast in a spectacular spot high in the mountains. Later we saw chinchilla, vicuna and a vulture. We reached the hotel in the evening. Mick and I took Pepé, Edwin and Raoul to dinner at Leonides, where we enjoyed the meal. A friend of Pepé's came in, a kayaker and guide. We discussed Sarah and her trip. Pepé said Sarah was not just a client but a journalist who was writing an article about the trip. He implied that she was allowed to go, despite her relative inexperience, because she was a *journalist. I was sceptical, thinking Amazonas Explorer, and other companies of course, would take anyone who could pay. We knew that young Chris, the last to be rescued from the raft Sarah was on, had no rafting experience at all.*

I wanted to be home. We set off for Lima on the 3rd and for home on the 4th, but we were delayed in Miami. Forty minutes into the British Airways flight to London, we were told we had to return to Miami as one engine had overheated. We flew around jettisoning fuel. Some people were frightened. I was not as I believed it was possible to fly with only one engine functioning. We spent the night at a good hotel in Miami, care of British Airways. Next day we flew home safely and were met by Matthew at Heathrow.

Barbara (First Year, Worst Year, Barbara A. Wilson, Wiley 2004)

So, we had survived the first year and the trek. Some people said to us, "Did it bring you peace?" or "Did it help you achieve closure?" a meaningless term to us. We did not achieve peace or closure. At the time we achieved emotional turmoil and physical exhaustion. The trip was something we felt we had to do. In retrospect, it was helpful to see what Sarah would have seen during her last days. We were pleased that, given she had to die, she was in such a beautiful place. We liked the valley and the ruins around. We felt her presence there although that may well have been wishful thinking. We continue to miss her, yearn for her, think about her and talk about her. We are still angry with her for going on the trip and causing us this anguish. We are sad that her nieces are left without their wonderful auntie. Rosie will always remember her, but Francesca will have nothing but the most fragmentary memories. We still have not been successful in getting a death certificate. We continue to be less bothered by the unimportant things in life, like missing a train or losing a belonging, and we still feel an immediate bond with any other parents who tell us they have lost a child."

We thought out hearts were broken when we lost our

firstborn child. Our hearts have healed, or at least the open wound has become a scar. We cry very readily. The disaster in the United States on September 11th affected almost all the world, but we felt particularly affected as we knew how parents losing adult children would feel, especially those who did not have a body to bury. Yet we felt their situation was worse than ours for men had caused the deaths of the people in New York, Washington, and Pennsylvania. Sarah chose her white-water rafting trip and was not the victim of brutality or terror. At times her death seems inevitable, at times we cannot really believe she is dead. We can laugh, enjoy ourselves, work, play, sleep, eat, despite this wound. The first year is hard, but as all bereaved parents say, "You learn to live with it". This is a cliché, but it is also true. Sarah, we miss you, we love you, we will never forget you. You were our joy, our treasure, our precious gift, and we will try to live our lives better because of you.

End

Lightning Source UK Ltd.
Milton Keynes UK
UKHW040941211021
392590UK00001B/16